To the students of the world;
young or otherwise.
We believe in you.

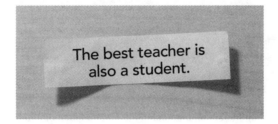

Contents

Foreword

Welcome to *Amplify*! As you will discover, this book totally rocks! Full of passionate and practical ideas for enhancing your teaching with technology, it stakes a rock-solid claim, grounded in research, for amplifying proven, constructivist teaching and learning strategies with technology. As Katie and Kristin make clear, it's not the technology but what we do with it that augments teaching and learning. "As digital tools became more and more present in our classrooms, we wanted to shy away from many of the practices that didn't make sense. Just because we *can* do something innovative, doesn't always mean we should." We get it. We've all seen the far-too-prevalent smartboards loaded with lame software that convert screens into fill-in-the-blank worksheets, or iPads stuffed with mind-numbing apps that differ little from the ditto packets reproduced in the copy rooms of yesteryear. You won't find them in this book. *Amplify* shares the collaborative journey of these two energetic risk takers as they open up their teaching and their kids' learning through the thoughtful use of technology. This book can help anyone who picks it up do the same. It certainly has me.

A number of years ago, I had the good fortune of working in Katie's and Kristin's classrooms at Burley School, in the Chicago Public Schools. Together with Smokey Daniels, principal Barbara Kent, and the amazing Burley staff, we worked to implement and sustain a school-wide, thoughtful, collaborative inquiry approach. Subsequent instructional videos featured Katie, Kristin, and their colleagues demonstrating extraordinary inquiry-based teaching. But technology was sparse. Katie, a born techie, had laptops in her room but little else. Kristin would peek in, curious about how tech platforms might enhance the learning in her first-grade classroom, but not entirely convinced. Together with their future-thinking tech whiz, Carolyn Skibba, they wrote and won an iPad grant and expanded on that over the next few years until their classrooms were "one-to-one," an iPad for every child.

But Katie and Kristin understood tech specialist Alan November's caution that one-to-one is a misnomer, that when we add devices it's one-to-world! Their kids were soon backchanneling with scientists in Antarctica, soliciting ideas from kids in Bremen, Germany on the best classroom pets, and getting global perspectives on climate change. Their contagious energy and passion lit up their one-to-world classrooms and ignited their kids' engagement and learning.

Just as Katie and Kristin fanned the flame of their kids' learning, they lit mine up too. And this book will light up yours. It's a perfect mix of theory and practice. Katie and Kristin know their stuff, and they fill us in on the research-based rationale for merging solid pedagogy with technology. But they also know that teachers need practical ideas for doing this work. At the end of chapters, they offer three things you can try tomorrow. How great is that! They share popular hashtags, apps, and websites for educators. They open up their mini-lesson structure and let you in on what a typical week can look like. In the independence chapter, they discuss the increasingly important idea of digital citizenship, the power of audience, and how to manage devices responsibly.

Most important, throughout the book they honor Don Graves' notion that teachers are the chief learners in the classroom. They recognize that the best teachers learn along with and also from their kids in all things but especially relative to technology. This kind of learning reveals a powerful way for kids to see that adults never stop trying new things, perhaps messing up, and ulti-mately learning from their attempts and from one another. Katie and Kristin also stress the power of collaboration among colleagues as they march forth on their pedagogical/technological expedition.

A lasting feature of this book is the ongoing discussion of what technology should and should not be. Katie and Kristin remind us that tech is not a silver bullet and does not supplant our traditional tools. They continue to put sticky notes and clipboards on their supply list. They don't abandon books or paper and pencils. They encourage a balance of digital text and print text, remind-ing us not to ignore print simply because tech is ubiquitous. Their kids read, write, and interact around conventional print, as well as digitally. *Amplify* builds a much needed bridge between powerful, research-based pedagogy and thoughtful technology use. Ultimately, this book urges us to open up a world of possibilities by giving our kids the widest possible range of tools, texts, and op-portunities for learning and wondering. Enjoy the ride. It's thrilling!

—Steph Harvey

Acknowledgments

Katie

@Burley3rdFloor You make me a better teacher and person. Thank you for your support, lunch every day, and spirited debates. #lovethetribe #sisters #staystrong

@BurleySchool I will miss you more than you know. Please burn the pictures, I know it wasn't karaoke night . . . I didn't care.

@Kons Thank you for your support, watching the toddler every weekend, and putting up with my creative moods. #loveofmylife

@Minime Watching you learn about life every day reminds me why I do this work and keeps me grounded. Please stop taking selfies with my phone. #evilgeniustoddler

@5bFish @HaleNetwork5th Your collaboration showed my students what it meant to be global learners. Here's to many more years of connecting our kids!

Kristin

@BigShouldersFund Josh, Rebecca, and Eliza, thank you for believing in me and agreeing to my crazy ideas! I couldn't ask for better colleagues. Your dedication to the students of Chicago is beyond measure. #Thisisschool

@SMOSChicago You fill my heart with joy and teach me every day. Thank you students and staff!

@Mark The adventure continues! #bestlifeever

@ADEfamily It's hard to imagine that in two years' time, one group of colleagues could have such an impact on who I am and what I believe. Thank you for pushing me to be more.

@**SaraKAhmed** You know. No words needed. See you on the #commoncourse #lifeinsidethecircle #HTR

@**Kimberly** Querrey Mentor and friend, you knew what I needed and helped me find it. You are the sister I choose.

Katie and Kristin

@**CarolynSkibba** Thank you for all of your support, encouragement, and amazing leadership! We are here because of YOU! #eduawesome #mentor #lovethetribe

@**StephHarvey** There are not enough words to thank you for all you've done. We stand on your shoulders, and that means everything. #mentorsrock

@**SmokeyDaniels** You are a friend, a mentor, an inspiration, and a believer. You make us better. #mentorsrock #literaturecircleswork

@**PrincipalBarbaraKent** Thank you for raising us as educators and for teaching us it all starts with a great book.

@**HeinemannTeam** You believed in us and our vision, thank you for taking us on this journey! #teacherPDmatters #PDLove

@**Holly** Thank you for your feedback and thoughtful critique, you helped us shape this project from a seed into a flower.

#**BurNTA, #nerdybookclub, #5thchat, #1stchat community** You've shaped ideas, given feedback that matters, and provided loads of laughter. Go forth and set the world on fire! #BurNTA4eva #ourkidsteach

Introduction

We invite you.

We invite you to join us on a journey to explore technology as a creative tool in your classroom. A tool that can amplify the learning and the work your students do. A tool that can be exciting and meaningful, connect us across the globe, and engage learners in innovative opportunities to learn, explore, and grow.

Technology-rich classrooms should bustle with the same amount of noise and collaborative energy we see when we look at elementary and middle school learners hard at work. Students move seamlessly between digital and nondigital formats as they read, write, talk, explore, and more. The scope of how and why students use technology is determined by teachers and students, working together to construct a learning environment that works best for everyone in the classroom. The goals: innovation, creativity, connection.

We invite you to join our tribe. A growing tribe of teachers who want more for their students than apps (applications) and programs and who dream bigger about what's possible with technology in the classroom. A group of educators who will work to ultimately define the role that technology plays in our students' lives, both in and out of the classroom. A group of teachers who believe that good teaching and technology are not mutually exclusive. If you believe that, then you're already a part of our tribe.

We grew up when "gaming" consisted of traveling the Oregon Trail and dying of dysentery shortly after trading your oxen for new wagon wheels. How times have changed, and drastically so. While we hear talk of "digital natives" and "digital immigrants," we recognize that tech tools have evolved throughout history, and today we find ourselves in another cycle of change. As was the case when society first was introduced to the ice box or the toaster, labels that define people as those who get it and those who don't fail to be helpful. Instead, we work to shift our mindset to reimagine what's possible. And that's exactly what makes this such an exciting time in education. We find ourselves between two worlds, one steeped in pedagogy and the other in technology, often wondering why the two so frequently pass each other by. We seek a bridge between these two worlds and are committed to bringing them together.

Digital learning is at a crossroads, and it's time for teachers and students to share our voices in how, why, and when our kids should use technology as a learning tool. We invite you to join us on a journey of discovery, exploration, and empowerment.

WHY WE DO THIS WORK

In a recent article in the *Washington Post* Kentaro Toyama writes about technology's Law of Amplification. He proposes that technology simply amplifies human forces and "in education, technologies amplify whatever pedagogical capacity is already there" (2015). This Law of Amplification is something that we have seen time and time again in our work and solidifies our belief that in order to use digital tools in a meaningful and innovative way we must first take into account strong pedagogy.

As digital tools became more and more present in our classrooms, we wanted to shy away from many of the practices that didn't make sense. Just because we *can* do something innovative or new doesn't always mean we should. We advocate for marrying new tools with what we already know is effective with students. We choose to ground our work with students in pedagogical research—taking what works in reading, writing, and math classrooms and enhancing that with tools at our disposal—instead of relying on specific software or programs, sales pitches or corporate-funded initiatives. It can be overwhelming to sift through educational technology tools and research. Whether navigating the eighty thousand apps curated for education or the start-up companies trying to win contracts for the "let us teach your kids" instructional program du jour, we feel there are far too many corporate voices and there is not enough educator and student input.

What we know about pedagogy guides us in teaching students to be self-directed learners. Show what you know. Represent your understanding. Create something. Teach others. We look beyond standards to gain a global perspective of how and why technology can and should shape the learning landscape that our students experience now and in the future. We challenge the notion that technology should be used for "sit and get" learning—a model still pervasive globally—instead of positioning students as critical thinkers and creators (Shear, Gallagher, and Patel 2011).

In a review of current research, Edutopia's Vanessa Vega (2013) identified three factors that signaled effective use of technology in the classroom. First, students were active learners and had access to feedback about their performance. Second, students actively analyzed and created media. Third, teachers leveraged tools to connect learning experiences in the classroom with the outside world. Teachers who utilized "innovative" teaching strategies better prepared students to develop skills needed for future work. These innovative teachers effectively blended face-to-face instruction with technology tools in a way that honors instructional practices proven to be effective. Essentially, layering technology with existing classroom instruction enhances what we do.

Over the years we've found the work of Dr. Ruben Puentedura to be instrumental in pushing our thinking on how technology can enhance learning in the elementary classroom. Most initial explorations into classroom technology use fall into the first level of his SAMR (substitution, augmentation, modification, redefinition) model. We first begin by replacing paper-and-pencil tasks with a technology tool (substitution). For example, students might type a list of books they have read instead of handwriting it, with the word processor replacing paper and pencil. As their knowledge of technology grows, teachers are able to augment instruction, which means that in addition to the technology serving as a substitution there is also some level of improvement in function. Connecting students' devices to the Internet gives them the ability to easily share their lists of books with teachers, parents, and each other via email, augmenting the original purpose of record keeping. Or perhaps students could use a more collaborative platform such as Google Drive so that teachers could monitor and support their work more closely. The next level in the model is modification.

At this level, technology becomes transformative and allows us to redesign the task. Now instead of typing the list of books they have read, students might use a digital Web tool—Goodreads, Shelfari, or Padlet, for example—to make their lists public and interactive. Lists are created for students by students, which can build community and excitement around reading lives. Lastly comes redefinition, where teachers can create entirely new tasks we never thought possible. Taking those digital tools a step further, students might not only keep a list of books they've read in a visual format but also collect links, personally recorded audio responses, and self-created digital media such as book trailers to share with their community.

For a more detailed explanation of the SAMR model, we encourage you to view Puentedura's podcasts (http://bit.ly/1JMHgeH) or visit his website at http://bit.ly/1MLKLll.

Puentedura and Vega's review of research remind us that when we bring technology into our classrooms, we must place emphasis on what our students will do with it. How will they create? How will they construct meaning? How will they connect the learning they do in the classroom with that of the real world? While many educators have focused on what people are calling personalized learning systems, we believe that true personalization comes when students have choice and input into how, why, and when they use technology.

GUIDING PRINCIPLES IN THIS BOOK

Based on current research and our years of experience with using technology in our own classrooms as well as working with teachers around the globe, we've established some guiding principles that drive this book.

An Emphasis on Student Ownership and Creativity

We want students to be the ones doing the work: creating, communicating, and learning. We place the highest value on technology use that encourages this practice. Although there are times when teachers are creating for students, these should not overshadow opportunities for students to create. Technology cannot stay locked away in a teacher's desk or computer lab; it must be accessible and used by every child in the room.

Technology Use That Is Heavily Tied to Literacy

Because technology tools can be powerful literacy tools that students use to write, talk, draw, capture, record, and interact, you will notice many instances of technology and literacy tightly woven together in this book. Technology tools have become part of our daily routines in reading and writing workshop and content literacy lessons. These areas prove to be some of the most innovative and exciting ones to enhance your instruction with tech tools.

Teacher Empowerment

We believe teachers can make the best decisions for their students. We want you to feel excited and passionate about using technology in your class, and if you're not quite there yet, we want you to gain a vision for where you'd like to go. We've tried to make our thinking visible and easy to follow so that what we're proposing feels not only manageable but inspiring.

Use of Gradual Release and Play Models

Do we carefully guide students step-by-step, modeling each skill as we slowly coach them toward independence, or do we let them play, explore, and discover? The answer is both. In this text we demonstrate that there are proper times to model essential skills for students in order to get them started, to show them how and why we do things, and to elevate the level of their work. However, we also believe that students can take the reins and discover so many things when it comes to technology in the classroom—why to use it, when to use it, how to use it in new and different ways. Then we turn the modeling and coaching over to them as they teach each other—and us!

WHAT YOU WILL FIND IN THIS BOOK

Getting started with meaningful technology involves a lot of working parts, so we organized this book into chapters that will support different areas of development. We wanted to offer both a big picture of teaching and learning with technology as well as some concrete lessons and examples that you can use tomorrow.

Chapter 1: Getting Started: Developing a Mindset for Using Technology

The first chapter of this book is designed to help the reader understand the mindset with which we need to approach technology use in the classroom. By keeping technology grounded in best practice and strong pedagogy, we can ensure that students' experiences will be meaningful and impact their learning outcomes.

Chapter 2: Journey of Discovery

In Chapter 2 we detail the many ways that you can reach out and connect with other educators to find effective tools, inspiring models, and new strategies. We also discuss the importance of embracing play and discovery in your own life as a means for professional growth and modeling for your students.

Chapter 3: Connecting Technology to Existing Classroom Practice

Chapter 3 gets into the details of how, why, and when we can and should use technology to enhance our classroom practices. Technology use doesn't mean that we throw out those strategies that we've found to be successful with students; it offers a way to enhance and add layers to our instruction.

Chapter 4: Foundational Lessons for Independence

One of the key elements of successful technology use is setting students up to be independent technology users. In this chapter you will find eleven lessons that we teach students each year to help them become responsible and independent technology users and digital citizens.

Chapter 5: Reflection and Assessment

Chapter 5 embraces the need for teachers and students to set aside time for reflection on and assessment of how technology is impacting the learning landscape of the classroom. This reflection is an essential component of understanding how we might better use the tools at our disposal to maximize our students' learning.

Chapter 6: Power Up for Connected Learning

In the last chapter of this book we share a wealth of ideas for using technology with your students. Organized into three sections—"Build Reading Communities," "Engage in Digital Discussions," and "Foster Inquiry Across the Curriculum"—this chapter is full of ways to get started right now!

Three Things to Try Tomorrow

We believe that it's important for you to have small steps that you can take, ideas that seem manageable. At the end of most chapters you will find a section that includes three things to try tomorrow. These are intended to be simple, straightforward, and easy to use with students right away. Just try!

Technology can be innovative and effective. It can and should be influenced by best practice, and your professional judgment is stronger than any sales pitch. We must also have the courage to try something new, to experiment, to move out of our comfort zone, to listen to our students, and to embrace a mindset that honors teachers' need to be creative, inspired, and joyful. Engage yourself in learning something new, find inspiration all around you, and empower your students to own the learning!

 Scan this QR code or visit http://hein.pub/amplify to see videos of teachers and students in action and access up-to-date resources for this book. (Enter your email address and password or click "Create a New Account" to set up an account. Once you have logged in, enter keycode AMPLIFY15 and click "Register.")

Getting Started

Developing a Mindset for Technology

In a semiquiet corner of Kristin's first-grade classroom, Wyatt sits down to reflect on his learning in the classroom recording booth. This homemade recording studio consisting of a laptop computer with a built-in webcam, a shower curtain from Target, an old desk, and some discarded pieces of packing foam serves as a place for students to record what they know, their reflections on their learning, and their passions and interests (see Figure 1.1).

Wyatt makes a silly face, takes a deep breath, and begins to record. "Hi! My name is Wyatt and I'm going to talk about Native Americans. I'll tell you about

Figure 1.1 Classroom Recording Booth

two tribes, the Pueblo and the Sioux. The Pueblo lived in adobes. I didn't know all that stuff when I was little, like when I was five or four. Now I know there's even more tribes than that!" He continues to talk about what he's learned during the unit and then shares a few new questions he has. "Well, that's all I have to say about this. Bye, 106!"

In another classroom, Katie sits, her fifth-grade students gathered close on the carpet, with her latest independent reading book in one hand and her iPad in the other. Today she is modeling how to do a vlog, or video blog, about a book.

"OK, everyone, I want you to watch carefully and listen as I record my vlog. I've practiced a few times to think through what I want to say, but I haven't written anything down. That's because I want this vlog to sound natural, like I'm talking right to my viewers. Jot some notes about what you see me doing in your notebook." She begins to record. "This is a sound test for my vlog." She stops the recording and plays it back. The students begin to take notes. "Right there, what did you notice me doing before I even got started? Turn and talk." Students turn to their partners and chat about what they noticed.

"I see her holding her iPad out in front of her so you can see her face," Alex says to Eli. "And she listened back to her recording."

"Yeah, I think that's a good idea," Eli replies, "because sometimes you do all your recording and then at the end you can't even hear it. That happened to me in math class last week and I had to do my recording again."

"OK, I hear some great things. Keep watching and jotting down your thoughts." Katie continues recording her vlog, which includes a quick review of her book and some of her thoughts about it. Students write down their thinking as she continues to model the process for them. She rerecords the review based on their comments.

"OK, readers, I think you're ready to go off and give it a try. Your book vlogs need to be posted on your blogs by the end of class today. Zack and Justin made a great video tutorial on the steps to take and posted it to their blog for you to use as a reference. Remember, you can always refer back to our anchor chart on making a book vlog [see Figure 1.2] if you have any questions. Have fun!"

These snapshots illustrate just some of the ways we enhance our classrooms with technology. They also reflect some of our core beliefs—our mindset—about teaching and learning: incorporate technology where it makes sense.

How to Make a Book Video Blog (Vlog)

* Set the scene; think about your background.

* Smile and greet your viewers.

* Show the cover of your book, with the title and author, as you introduce it.

* Give other important details: part of a series? genre? length?

* Tell us about the book—share what happens and your thinking/opinions.

* Speak loudly and clearly so your audience can hear you.

* Listen back to make sure everything sounds good before you post it.

* Show it to a friend for feedback.

Figure 1.2 Book Vlog Anchor Chart

These video recordings transform how we assess our developing readers and writers. When our students record a video reflection, we get a clear picture of what they've learned, questions they have, and how they're building knowledge around a topic. Far exceeding the information a standardized test score might convey, a video of a student talking about his or her learning is the feedback we need to plan tomorrow's instruction. Kids like to talk; when we open the door for them to do so, we get a great deal of insight into them as learners, thinkers, communicators, and people. Technological tools provide additional information when we are attempting to discern what students know and are able to do. Audio and video recordings help us analyze where understanding breaks down. By using this information to drive our instruction, we can meet our students' needs more than ever before.

CORE PRINCIPLES THAT DRIVE INSTRUCTION

No matter what devices or resources we have, we let our core beliefs and mindset guide how we use tools in the classroom. We focus on the overall goal of teaching kids how to think and then layer in purposeful tools along the way.

The term tools *does not always refer to technology tools. Tools are anything that we use in our instruction to support students, ranging from pencils, sticky notes, colored markers, and clipboards to projectors, tablets, and computers.*

We—and our students—need to understand how the tools work and why we're using them. In order to do that, we need to remind ourselves what effective teaching looks like and fall back on the work of teacher-researchers and authors who have guided our teaching. In the early days, it was rare to see either one of us without a copy of Fountas and Pinnell's *Guiding Readers and Writers* (2000). Over the years, we've expanded our list of professional texts and now we stand on the shoulders of those who've come before us. The work of Stephanie Harvey, Anne Goudvis, Harvey "Smokey" Daniels, Ellin Keene, Nancy Atwell, Lucy Calkins, Ralph Fletcher, Matt Glover, Penny Kittle, Teri Lesesne, Debbie Miller, and Pat Cunningham has shaped how we teach reading and writing workshop. More recently we've been inspired and influenced by Donalyn Miller, Chris Lehman and Kate Roberts, Kristi Mraz, Stephanie Parsons, Meenoo Rami, Franki Sibberson, and Sara Ahmed. This next generation of authors and thinkers continues to innovate as the conditions for learning evolve.

We keep these leaders and established best practices, which are research based, teacher tested, and kid approved, at the core of all we do. When introducing technological tools, we apply the same practices and strategies we use in reading and writing workshop. We model what we want students to do with the technology and guide them to try it out with us. We then provide ample time for students to practice on their own, experiment, and share as a class, thus building new knowledge collaboratively.

Use a Workshop Model for Instruction

The workshop is a predictable instructional model that provides students time in which to interact. It supports an "interdependent, interpersonal community in which children with particular knowledge and skills teach others" (Calkins, Tolan, and Ehrenworth 2010, viii). Technology in the classroom fits easily into this hands-on approach to learning: our students should be the ones using it. Because the format of minilessons, guided practice, independent practice, and debriefing is familiar to students, it is easy for them to jump in and focus on the task at hand. Oftentimes we combine this structure with unstructured experimentation by allowing students some time to play with a new tool before the lesson begins. Figure 1.3 outlines a possible lesson introducing a new piece of technology to the class.

Hold Small-Group and Individual Conferences

Students acquiring technological skills excel or struggle in various way, much as they do with any subject. Conferring with them not only about content but also about digital tools supports their budding skills. We start with compliment conferences to establish an atmosphere where we value student strengths, encourage risk taking, and help students understand their own areas of expertise (Serravallo and Goldberg 2007). We name specific, observable things students are doing well that they can repeat in the future. In later conferences we push students' thinking about their work, ask them to push themselves, and always circle back to the compliments to help them see where they are finding success.

Play	5 minutes	Give students a few minutes to log in or open the tool and explore. Guide them by asking, "What do you notice? What do you think you can do with it? What other tools does it remind you of?"
Minilesson	10–15 minutes	Explicitly model the skills needed to get started or that are essential. "Today we are going to use this tool to _____. There are many great things to learn about it, but to get you started I want to be sure you understand how to _____."
Guided and Independent Practice	30–45 minutes	Coach students in starting to use the tool, employing support methods such as turn-and-talks and conferences. When students are ready, send them off to work independently. As they work, help them and encourage them to help one another. The goal is always to promote independence, not dependence: • "Let me show you; then you can be our classroom specialist." • "I'm not sure; let's figure it out together." • "Check with [classmate's name]; she knows how to do that well."
Debriefing	5–10 minutes	Gather students so they can share what they have learned. Capture their new knowledge on a chart they can refer to during future work sessions. • "What tips or tricks did you learn today?" • "What were you successful at and what was challenging?" • "What innovations did you come up with today?"

Figure 1.3 Applying the Workshop Model to Learning a New Tool

We confer with students one-on-one or in small groups (Lucy Calkins calls the latter "table conferences"). Oftentimes a personalized teaching point for one will benefit the group, and we naturally invite students seated nearby into the conference. We typically try to ask questions of students while conferring: we believe an effective conference guides kids to do most of the talking and thinking. These questions also help us decide which points to focus on during coaching. Figure 1.4 lists some examples of teacher language during conferences.

Complimenting	Questioning	Coaching
• I noticed you are organizing some information in your notebook before you begin exploring your tech tool; that's a very thoughtful strategy. • The titles and subtitles you are using in your digital project help me understand what you are doing. • The images you are creating are so realistic. You include all the little details about the animals mentioned in the story. When you share this, I think everyone will know exactly what you have drawn.	• Can you tell me more about why you chose to do this? • What have you discovered so far? • Is there anything that you are finding challenging right now? • How are you using the tool to expand on what you normally would have done? • What are you trying to accomplish with this project? • What are you planning to do next?	• I see what you are trying to do here; let me show you a quicker way. • Have you thought about trying _____? • Maybe we could go back to our mentor example and look for ideas. • I'd like you to walk around the room and get a feel for how other people are approaching their projects. • What if we tried it like this? • Let's go back and look at our anchor chart for the lesson. Maybe that will help. • Say more about that. • Talk that through.

Figure 1.4 Examples of Language We Use When Conferring with Students About Technology

Engage Kids in Cross-Curricular Content

Visitors to Kristin's first-grade classroom often ask, "What subject is this?" Her favorite answer is "Thinking"; she's pleased that it's not obvious whether it's reading, writing, or science. When you see her students spread out on the floor, creating large murals, books scattered about them, paint everywhere, sentence strips cut into label-sized pieces, working together, it's clear that they are doing all three of these subjects and more. We advocate for a curriculum that teaches kids how to think and problem solve effectively. If we can teach students to do that, they can tackle any subject or curriculum we put in front of them.

Connecting various content areas is a powerful way to learn. Students deeply engage as they read, write, talk, view, watch, explore, create, and interact around a topic they have ideally had a voice in choosing (Zemelman, Daniels, and Hyde 2012). Cross-curricular learning goes beyond a simple theme; students meaningfully explore a topic from various angles, then synthesize that information into a deeper understanding. Whether these experiences are connected to a mandated unit or a more authentic inquiry, technology provides valuable enhancements to the work we ask students to do (see Figure 1.5). We encourage you to work with colleagues to make thoughtful choices about when to use strategies that include technology and when to use strategies that don't.

Scaffold Learning

The gradual release of responsibility is present often in our classrooms; it becomes a predictable scaffold for how the learning sequence will unfold. Students adopt it as a habit for learning and as a result don't feel anxious about when they will get a turn: they focus on the instructional portion of the lesson, knowing that in a few minutes they'll have the chance to talk about it and try it out.

Use Anchor Charts to Support Learners

As we introduce technology tools, we do what we can to make students' interactions with them positive. We want kids to gain skills with an application or a device, enjoy the experience, and be eager to try again and learn more in the future. One way we support our students is by creating anchor charts that use pictures, diagrams, and symbols to guide them through a process. As Marjorie

Without technology, students . . .	With technology, students can . . .
<ul><li>listen to read-alouds about the topic.</li><li>gather a bin of books for independent study.</li><li>read articles about the topic.</li><li>view and analyze images.</li><li>discuss the topic with their classmates face-to-face.</li><li>discuss materials in written conversation.</li><li>take a field trip, if feasible.</li><li>explore models or artifacts.</li></ul>	<ul><li>listen to audiobooks about the topic.</li><li>gather online resources to add to their study.</li><li>read material on websites, including primary source documents.</li><li>view and analyze high-quality color images and media clips.</li><li>discuss the topic with their classmates and students in other classes and schools via a digital platform.</li><li>Skype, email, or tweet with an expert.</li><li>take a virtual field trip.</li></ul>

Figure 1.5 Strategies That Don't Use Technology Versus Those That Do

Martinelli and Kristine Mraz note in *Smarter Charts* (2012), a picture really *is* worth a thousand words and is faster to read! These multilayered charts guide students through successful interactions with technology, providing the support that helps them do just a little bit more than they would be able to do on their own and that ultimately leads to independence. The charts we and our students create together might list kid-safe search engines, describe what a good blog comment looks and sounds like, display common icons used on digital platforms, or explain online collaboration tools. They hang in our classrooms and are uploaded to our websites, accessible to students whenever and wherever they need them.

Experiment with Digital Instruction and Visual Aids

Technology enables us to capture and archive our teaching in ways never before possible. We use tech tools to archive charts, organizers, and other handouts in a way that students and parents can access with ease. We use videos and screen captures to take snapshots of our teaching for students who may need a review at their fingertips. These reviews can be process oriented, such as a tutorial on how to share a project, or content based, as in a personalized minilesson or modeling video.

Students can take charge and create their own digital supports. For example, we encourage students to curate their own learning by archiving digital images with annotations of the concepts they want to remember. (See Chapter 5 for more information.) These personalized digital study guides encourage them to take charge of their own learning.

Adapt the Content

Technology offers many options for assisting students. Websites have texts that can be manipulated to varied levels of difficulty. Students can access audiobooks or teacher-created recordings of texts. Teachers have the ability to create resources that are specific to their students and classrooms (see Figure 1.6). Technology tools have such a wide range of uses when it comes to meeting the needs of every learner in the classroom. Through repetition, adaptation, curation, and connections, every student can get just the right amount of support he or she needs to find success.

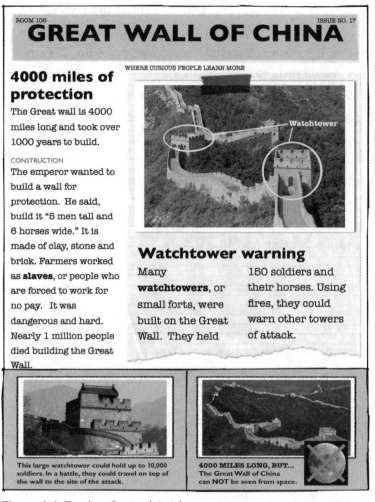

Kristin summarizes information from a more advanced text and puts it into student-friendly language. A layout program enables her to use nonfiction features to make it both informative and engaging.

Figure 1.6 Teacher-Created Article

Encourage Collaboration and Conversation

To prepare our students for today and tomorrow's world, we must engage them in collaborative learning. In the modern workplace, teams of people come together to solve problems. Tapping into the collective knowledge and intelligence of the group energizes involvement and expands ideas (Nichols 2006). We value this collaboration and acknowledge the powerful support students provide one another in group settings, whether in a face-to-face turn-and-talk or via mobile devices. Chatting digitally makes students' thinking visual, helps them form responses, and lets them build on one another's ideas. It also lets us be present in many discussions at once (Harvey et al. 2013).

Drive Instruction with Assessment

Good teachers make instructional decisions based on what we know about the students sitting in front of us. Each child enters our classroom with different passions, personality, and abilities. We get to know students as individuals so we can nudge them along the continuum of learning. We use feedback from our students to plan future instruction. From day one we immerse ourselves in the recursive loop of assessment and instruction.

Once we assess students we use this information to plan tomorrow's instruction. We match our instruction to student needs by planning minilessons, conferring with small groups and individuals, and providing rich resources. Then we assess again and gather more data to make sure our lessons and feedback are promoting learning. Because this assessment cycle is ubiquitous, it's hard to determine whether we are assessing to evaluate our instruction or instructing based on our assessments, and that's exactly what we want. Every response we get from students—their sticky notes, thinksheets (2-column charts or graphic organizers, for example), video snapshots, conversations, blog posts—contains data we value and use to plan future learning.

START WITH WHAT MAKES SENSE

Several years ago, Katie and her husband traveled to Italy. They spent a weekend eating their way through Rome, and on the last evening set off to find the best pizza place in the city. Guidebook in hand, they ventured behind Vatican City into a nontouristy neighborhood. Arriving at a hole-in-the-wall restaurant, their eyes bulged. Giant square pans lined the counter, holding pizza after pizza, golden crusts bubbling. Using what little Italian they knew, they tried to identify the toppings on each pie, with little success. Finally, Katie pointed at random—and they gorged themselves on piping hot, deliciously fresh slices of heaven. As they were finishing the last scrumptious bites, the cook brought out five new pans with entirely different pizzas! They debated whether to sample another round, but decided not to as they had to head back to the piazza—and anyway, they were too full for even one more bite.

We could gorge ourselves on technology tools as well if we chose to. So many choices—platforms, devices, apps—leave us wondering where to begin and feeling that as soon as we master one thing, there will be another new thing to learn. The important thing is to get started. Once you build momentum, see your students' excited reactions, and begin to find success, you'll be encouraged to try more and more tools in your classroom!

When we consider where to start, these questions guide our decisions:

- What tools do we have access to and how do they fit into our existing learning environment?
- Who are our students and what do they need? How can technology help them address those needs?
- How do we get started?

What Tools Do We Have Access To and How Do They Fit into Our Existing Learning Environment?

Equipment constraints are often our first concern: how can we use technology when we don't have any? The good news is that we can accomplish a lot with only a few devices—or sometimes just one. Once we have a vision for how technology might fit into our classroom, it becomes much easier to articulate what we need and why to stakeholders.

Think about the typical elementary learning environment. Students are seated in small groups so they can better collaborate on tasks and interact with one another. There is a large classroom library with comfortable places for students to snuggle up and read. There is a whole-class meeting area with a large carpet, a comfortable couch or chair, and an easel or a board. Technology should fit into this environment seamlessly, not detract from our comfortable and collaborative spaces. Here are some options:

- Rather than have a computer table, position computers around the room. Place one on a low table or bookshelf with a pillow nearby to sit on.
- Purchase lap desks students can use to support tablets while lying on the floor or sitting in small groups. Establish clear expectations for device safety.

- Place your projection screen so students can view it from their tables and the whole-class meeting area.
- If you have the option, choose devices that encourage student use and collaboration and that provide access to as many students as possible. (For example, choose several tablets instead of one interactive whiteboard.)

We're often asked, "What is the most transformative piece of technology in your classroom?" The items that initially transformed our classrooms were a laptop computer and a projector. A computer initiates the idea of mobile learning and opens the classroom to the world. Once we are able to project images from a computer, sharing websites and videos with the entire class becomes a regular part of the day. A document camera and a set of speakers complete the must-have ensemble. With a document camera we can project student work, zoom in on sections of text from books we want to share, and display high-quality color images of just about anything we need the class to see. After that, you can add more computers, tablets, iPads, and other devices a few at a time. The technology is as transformational as we make it. It's not the tool that counts; it's what we do with it.

Who Are Our Students and What Do They Need?

Each day we observe our students sitting on the rug and think about each one. Who sticks out? *If only Max would read. If only Brandy would participate more. If only I could get Tina excited.* If only . . . Technology by itself won't fix these issues, but it can open doors for students and give them an entry point into learning. The opening vignettes of this chapter demonstrate how we used video to meet a need in our classrooms. We wanted to know what students could do when they weren't limited by their ability to express themselves in writing. For Kristin's first graders, who were all developing writers, this opportunity was transformative. Kristin was able to determine what her students knew and were able to do without having to confer with each one individually. Katie wanted to help students capture their blogging voice and understand the personal and personable way blogs connect writers to their audience. Many students were writing very formal book reviews, and the vlog helped them find a more natural voice and eventually apply it to their written posts.

How Do We Get Started?

The key to getting started is to jump in with something small that you can use right away. You want to be able to take deliberate, manageable steps, like a runner training for a marathon (or, for some of us, a 5K!). A tool you can use tomorrow involves no student logins or accounts, requires minimal equipment, and connects to the day's learning goals. It should also make sense within the scope of best-practice teaching and extend or enhance students' learning. Figure 1.7 summarizes what technology should (and shouldn't) do for your classroom.

Technology should . . .	Technology shouldn't . . .
• provide opportunities for differentiated assessment. • give students access to authentic audiences. • increase the collaborative nature of lessons and group work. • diversify the resources to which students have access. • enable long-term archiving for reflection and assessment.	• be a silver bullet. • replace the teacher. • supplant traditional tools like clipboards and markers; it's just another option. • be used only for formal assessments. • be used by students in isolation.

Figure 1.7 What Technology Should and Shouldn't Do

Three Things to Try Tomorrow

Online Reading

Every morning, Katie's fifth graders pour into her classroom excitedly, talking about their previous evening as they unpack bags and get ready for their day. As they settle in, they carefully retrieve their iPads from the storage cart and find reading nooks around the room. On some mornings there's a URL written on the board for a special website or article that Katie wants them to read; on other mornings students choose from sources like *National Geographic Kids* (kids.nationalgeographic.com), *Sports Illustrated Kids* (sikids.com), or *Smithsonian TweenTribune* (tweentribune.com). Katie also provides a wide variety of nonfiction print: a large informational text section in the classroom library, bins of books relating to science or social studies units, a class subscription to a current events magazine, and various single copies of student-friendly magazines. Reading nonfiction first thing in the morning is a way for students to settle into their day and increases both the daily minutes they spend reading and the amount of informational reading they do. Before moving into the day's minilesson, students respond to their nonfiction reading in a variety of ways. Sometimes it's a quick check-in on a digital form or a brief online conversation on the classroom social network. Other times they chat in person with a partner or in a small group.

> Note that online reading does not replace the time that students read self-selected titles. We make time in our schedules by removing nonessential busywork in order to offer additional reading minutes to add these digital experiences.

Daily reading is an essential component of the elementary classroom. A healthy balance of student- and teacher-selected texts, comprehension instruction, and many opportunities to practice reading creates strong readers. Research is clear that minutes spent reading equal student achievement (Nagy, Herman, and Anderson 1985). By intentionally providing time for digital reading, we invite students to learn about current events and topics of interest. A balanced approach works best, based on interest, curricular inquiry, and classroom learning experiences.

Students benefit from explicit instruction in applying navigation and comprehension strategies when reading in a digital format. Although it's tempting to label students as digital natives and assume they understand these concepts, it's clear that kids need support, and it's up to us to explicitly teach and model elements of digital reading. We teach skills like scrolling and navigating, the functions of different Web elements, minimizing distractions, and finding just-right websites (Harvey et al. 2013).

Starting Points

- Dedicate time to Web reading. Whether a few times a week or every day, give students time to practice their online reading skills. Alternate between having students choose sites or articles to read and assigning shared texts.
- Examine your current units of study. Where might you incorporate some Internet resources or reading opportunities? Find at least one article or website that will enrich students' understanding and diversify their resources.
- Build on students' passions and curiosity. Use online reading to follow up on students' questions and wonderings—those connected to a unit of study or a book they've read or simply a question a student has a burning desire to answer.

Recording Booth

A class recording booth is one of the easiest ways to capture student thinking. You can create a recording booth with practically any device—laptops, smartphones, tablets, and Chromebooks all have built-in cameras that will allow you to capture video. Once you have a device, find a quiet corner in your classroom and start recording! It's that simple. (See Harvey et al. [2013].)

We find that most devices with built-in cameras have some form of recording program available by default. A few possibilities include Camera, Apple's iMovie, or WeVideo. Choose something simple to use and focus on how the tool can capture a different type of evidence. Often what kids say gives us completely different information than a written response. We depend on the recording booth so much that we've added a microphone to eliminate interference from background noise: we need to capture their thinking in a high-quality format.

There are many options for using a recording booth. We have students summarize and synthesize their learning at the end of a curricular inquiry. Asking kids to talk about what they know provides the opportunity for a strengths model assessment. We also use the recording booth for video book reviews, which we make accessible to students as a means for sharing reading recommendations.

Video book reviews create a book buzz (Miller 2009) as students excitedly talk about their favorite books and make plans for future reading. By allowing kids to record video book reviews and making them accessible on a website or blog ("Why don't you go watch the latest book videos and get some ideas about what to read next?"), we build a community in which kids know they have an audience for their work.

We use video recording across all subjects! Kristin's students take their math manipulatives into the recording booth and explain and demonstrate how to solve a complex math problem. Watching a student's math process, from setup to solution, gives her different information than she gets from reviewing a student's written computations. With thirty-two students, it's difficult for Katie to meet with book clubs as frequently as she would like. When she isn't able to be present for the meeting, she sets up a camera to record the students' interactions. This window into the thinking and learning taking place helps her get up to speed and participate in the next group meeting. It also helps her assess the group members' collaboration skills—how they interact and build their thinking together.

Starting Points
- Start by modeling for students what the video should look like. This will help you maximize time spent recording and avoid many videos that make you motion sick from the camera lurching violently to and fro.
- Set up your device in a corner of the classroom so students have a quiet place to record their thinking. Add supports like a chart depicting how to start, record, and stop the camera. To ensure you capture ideas from

all students, post a class roster in the booth; when one student finishes her recording, she crosses her name off the list and lets the next child on the list know it's his turn. To decorate your recording studio, add a colorful shower curtain, piece of fabric, or even a green screen. A solid background hides activity in the classroom so the student making the video is less distracted and viewers can focus on the speaker. If background noise is an issue, add an external microphone like a Snowball USB mic or use headphones with a built-in microphone.

Digital Bulletin Boards

We use a variety of simple-to-access, digital collaborative spaces to gather feedback from students, respond to student work, or provide information and site links. Like corkboards, chart paper, and sticky notes that make thinking visible, these digital collaborative spaces invite all students to view, respond, and interact. There are other good tools available, but we like Padlet because it has a number of options, is accessible from numerous devices, provides a personalized URL, is easy to share, and saves all bulletin boards in a single account. It's a wonderful tool for gathering feedback from students; we often use it to pull together final thoughts about a lesson or to share lingering questions. It's quick to set up and easy for students to access and thus the perfect tool for impromptu lessons and data collection.

When Kristin's class finished a read-aloud of *The Little Red Hen*, she created a Padlet wall that said, "Did the Little Red Hen do the right thing? Share your thinking." (See http://bit.ly/1TdZ46J.) The notes kids added led to a wonderful debate on what is fair. Katie has used it in a similar way to archive students' thinking, as a place for student book clubs to share their learning, to collect exit tickets after a lesson, and as a format for students to create their own websites.

Starting Points

- If you have only a few devices, set up your digital board and leave it displayed and ready. Have students visit during the workshop to share their thinking about a current read-aloud or how they applied the day's minilesson. This is a great way to engage them in reflection and works as a formative assessment piece for you.

- Set up a number of walls by genre or category. Students can leave book reviews on the appropriate wall, as well as get suggestions for books to read. Padlet walls support images, videos, and links. You can also generate QR (Quick Response) codes (scannable barcodes that can direct a user to a specific website) that can be scanned by devices and which will take students directly to the site.

TAP INTO YOUR PASSION

No matter what, find your passion and bring it into the classroom. Kristin was passionate about connecting her young readers with authors. They loved their daily independent reading and yearned to talk with the authors of their favorite books, so she made that happen using Skype (a video chat application). She knew writing letters to the authors would be challenging for her first graders, so Skype was the perfect medium for them to see the face of a real live author, who later became a classroom celebrity. (See Chapter 6 for more information on connecting with authors digitally.)

Katie's passion is blogging. She began her teaching blog many years ago as a way to reflect on her practice and connect with other educators. She discovered that writing the blog entries made her more thoughtful about the steps she took in the classroom as she pushed herself to articulate the importance of choices she made. When other teachers started reading and commenting, she found the interaction with her peers exciting and invigorating. Might her students gain the same energy and inspiration by being part of a blogging community? Katie decided to give them the same opportunity to connect digitally on a simple blog about books. Students took turns posting book reviews each week. As she became a more experienced blogger and was able to bring more devices into her classroom, she helped her students create their own blogs on which they shared their reading, curricular inquiries, mathematical thinking, and writing. Today they participate in worldwide blogging communities and connect with student bloggers from Kuala Lumpur, Malaysia, to Reykjavik, Iceland.

Our technology skills evolve over time, but we have to begin with one small step. It doesn't matter where we are on that continuum, only that we've placed ourselves in the exciting world of digital learning. Once you've begun, commit to taking one step forward each quarter of the school year—by doing so you'll know how to use four tools by the end of the year. A year later, you'll have eight options for engaging students and capturing thinking. Chances are, you'll learn more than one new thing each quarter and quickly will have a wide-ranging set of resources and tools at your fingertips.

 Scan this QR code or visit http://hein.pub/amplify to see videos of teachers and students in action and access up-to-date resources for this book (use keycode AMPLIFY15).

Journey of Discovery

Kristin knows the power of discovery firsthand. She believed strongly in the social skills needed for learning—interaction, collaboration, response—and was hesitant to bring technology into her classroom. She imagined a small child, eyes glazed, headphones on, working in isolation, staring blankly at a computer screen, mindlessly clicking through a letter recognition game, à la Space Invaders. This was not the type of experience she wanted her students to have.

In 2008 Kristin traveled to the Louisiana Bayou on an Earthwatch Educator Fellowship to research climate change post–Hurricane Katrina alongside a team from Tulane University. One requirement for the trip was that she would hold video conferences with her students in Chicago several times during the week. Via Skype, Kristin's first graders traveled to the bayou. They were amazed by the bunkhouse on stilts where Kristin lived with seven other teachers. They asked about the cypress trees, the alligators, and the caterpillars that the team collected, as they watched scientists and their teacher interact with the environment in real time. Back in Chicago, these six-year-olds researched the swamp ecosystem and, clipboards poised, conferred with the research team's PhD students and professors. By using technology to connect her class to expert scientists in the field, Kristin gave her students something she alone wasn't able to provide. Simply talking on her classroom rug about what it means to be a scientist wouldn't have had the profound impact that this authentic experience provided them.

By the time Kristin returned to Chicago, the students had gathered local leaf samples, written books about invasive species, and championed the endangered brown pelican. Virtually bringing her students to the bayou ignited a passion in them to learn something new. Most important, they had access to experts and new resources that they had previously not known. For Kristin this experience showed her the power of technology and she began to explore ways to connect her students to the outside world all year long. Taking a risk and trying something paid off and she saw how the experience prompted students to think bigger about their learning. Today she uses FaceTime and Google Hangouts in addition to Skype to give her students regular video access to authors, experts, and other students around the world.

DISCOVERY AND EVERYDAY WONDERS

Where do you make discoveries in your life? Do you comb the bookstore, looking for information on the latest travel destinations? Play in the kitchen with new recipes? Attempt a different workout routine?

We've long known that to be excellent reading teachers, we must be readers. To hone our skills as writing teachers, we must write. And to elevate our ability to problem solve, we need to engage in critical thinking and analysis.

As teachers, we are the chief learners in the room. We live curiously with our students, exploring books, artifacts, and curriculum with a sense of wonder.

We embrace inquiry as we investigate a snowflake, explore the solar system, or help a student research the answer to a question. We learn about our craft and constantly try new things in the classroom, reflecting, talking, and ultimately adjusting our practice. When we want to know more about reading workshop, we read books, watch videos of teachers and students in action, talk with colleagues, and go to conferences. We do the same with writing workshop, math, science, and social studies. We seek out experts and specialists as our mentors. Technology is just another layer of professional learning we need to embrace. We challenge you to explore within your personal and professional lives in order to inspire yourself and your students!

School Cohorts

We are strong believers in homegrown learning. Whom better to learn from and with than the people we teach alongside every day? It's essential to build a strong culture of professional learning with our colleagues so we can analyze how we use technology, give one another feedback, brainstorm ideas, and play together! Collectively we have a wide range of experience. Through discussion and exploration, we can tap into everyone's expert opinions and create a program that works for our students. Here are two ways to get started:

1. *Hold a professional book study.* Teachers who read together learn together. We've experienced firsthand how a shared vision can guide a faculty or group of teachers to next steps and new learning. Our former principal in the Chicago Public Schools, Barbara Kent, led the staff through a collaborative book study each year along with a team of teacher-leaders. Book by book, we gained new skills, engaged in healthy discourse, and challenged our instructional practices. We tested new lessons in our classrooms, analyzed student work samples, and identified successes and gaps in our instruction. Professional book study is a catalyst for innovation and a necessity for gaining a common language throughout a school.

2. *Choose one thing to explore together.* We credit our colleague, Carolyn Skibba, with nearly all we've learned about technology and we believe her instructional style can (and should!) be replicated. Carolyn nudges her staff to embrace technology by trying or adopting one new tool at

a time. Instead of overwhelming teachers with everything they need to know about technology, Carolyn helps teachers explore one relevant tool they can use right away in their curriculum. She meets with grade-level teams and hosts weekly drop-in tech meetings: teachers stop by during their lunch hour and spend twenty minutes investigating a new tool. Once teachers discover something new, the buzz quickly spreads throughout the building; people test it or ask questions so they can learn more. This nonthreatening exploration encourages teachers to take a risk and try something new. Teachers, in collaboration, think about how these tools can be used to build student thinking, which makes it feel manageable.

Online Learning and Social Media

To connect with people around technology, it's important to go where the techies go. Teachers at all levels of expertise participate in social media groups and take online classes. Technological experts conduct webinars to share ideas and new learning. Social media websites like Twitter, Facebook, and Google+ encourage a sense of community. Digital communities such as the Educator Collaborative focus on various aspects of classroom practice through small groups.

Webinars

Attending a webinar—a sixty- to ninety-minute online video conference—is a convenient way to gain new knowledge right from your favorite reading chair. Participating in webinars is often cheaper than physically attending a conference, and most have some type of interactive feature—a chat room or back channel in which participants converse, ask questions, and interact with the presenter and other attendees using a social media tool. Webinars that explore a topic deeply are usually more satisfying than those that advertise a lot of content ("fifty apps in fifty minutes"). Find something that feels manageable and provides new learning you can use with your students. A variety of professional organizations and publishers offer webinars for educators. Here are three good places to start: Heinemann (http://bit.ly/1L3pRAe), the Association for Supervision and Curriculum Development (ASCD) (http://bit.ly/1fs3FwH), and the International Society for Technology in Education (ISTE) (http://bit.ly/1e5WDDq).

Teacher Blogs

Isolation is the enemy of professional learning. Teaching is a social profession, but we can often find ourselves working for days without ever speaking to another adult! We know the value of collaboration and practice it daily with our students; the same is true for us as professionals. We learn more, think differently, and do better when we have regular access to others who help us reflect on our craft and discover new opportunities.

One of the best ways to start a discovery journey is by investigating what other teachers have done in their classrooms. Teacher websites and blogs are created by colleagues in the thick of teaching and learning every day, who, like us, are trying to use what they have in the best way they know how. They are experimenting, documenting, reflecting, sharing their classroom practice, hoping for feedback, and connecting with other teachers in an effort to improve their instruction. Followers are often able to examine student work, see videos of a classroom in action, and discover the teacher's thought process in relation to what's happening. It's challenging to open one's teaching to scrutiny but doing so is an essential part of becoming a reflective professional.

Our current favorites are linked on our blog, http://bit.ly/1S7StJy (a screenshot of the home page is shown in Figure 2.1), but blogs and links change quickly. The following websites publish a list of top educator blogs:

EdTech **magazine:** "The 2014 Honor Roll: EdTech's Must-Read K–12 IT Blogs" (http://bit.ly/YejeVX)

Teach.com: "Teach100" (http://bit.ly/Z6sbkY)

The Edublog Awards: (http://bit.ly/1ucFQiK)

eSchool News: "Ten Follow-Worthy Education Blogs" (http://bit.ly/1B95y0W)

Social Media

Teachers are now able to connect with colleagues around the globe who want to improve their practice. Social media encourages teachers in all parts of the world to collaborate and spend time in one another's classrooms. Tools like Twitter and Google+ make it easy to plan and share lesson ideas and find new applications and resources. The more professionals we connect with, the better

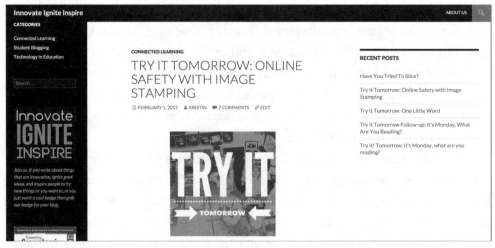

Figure 2.1 Screenshot of Our Blog's Home Page

able we are to find ideas, get feedback, and build excitement for new uses of technology in our classrooms. Start by creating a Twitter account and following some educators you admire. Over time the number of people you follow will grow. If you're not yet ready for Twitter, sites like Classroom 2.0 (http://bit .ly/1gN5YuB) and the Educator Collaborative Community (http://bit.ly/1niQUfC) offer slower-paced forums.

Conferences

Thousands of education conferences are held each year, and they can be a wonderful catalyst for discovery. Ranging from the very large (ISTE's annual conference has more than sixteen thousand attendees) to small, intimate teacher meetups, conferences are places to wonder, explore, and connect with other educators. Whether you go with a team of learners from your school or alone, don't pass up an opportunity to attend a conference.

Organizations like the International Literacy Association bring in well-known speakers from all over the world. Large conferences are a kind of tasting menu—you get to sample many different entrees and develop your palate, but you're often hungry for more. These types of events give you a feel for what's out there but can be overwhelming, so go with a plan: identify a few key people you want to see. Most professional organizations also have smaller-scale work-shops, social events, or tweetups (a face-to-face meetup with your Twitter PLN) where it's much easier to interact. If you're just looking to connect with like-minded educators, seek out a special-interest or small-group meetup.

On the opposite end of the continuum from a national conference is the regional conference, local chapter meeting, or Edcamp. These meetings are usu-ally created by teachers, for teachers, as opportunities to collaborate and build understanding around a smaller idea. This is where you build your personal learning network (PLN). Attendees have shared needs, common interests, and a range of expertise. Topics vary by grade and subject and are often fluid and flexible. These settings are more intimate and educators are able to dig deeper into an idea or practice. Edcamps, which cost little to nothing to attend, are a great way to explore something new or outside your typical subject area. (To learn what Edcamps are and how to organize one, visit the Edcamp Foundation at http://bit.ly/1GvYtbg; to search for upcoming Edcamps in your area, visit the foundation's wikispace at http://bit.ly/1B5J54U.)

A new trend in teacher collaboration is the "unconference"—a teacher workshop with no set agenda that provides educators a space to work and create. In 2013, Kristin's colleagues Jennie Magiera, Autumn Laidler, and Sue Gorman left a tech conference unsatisfied: they'd been introduced to a number of new technology tools but hadn't had time to explore them in depth. This prompted their idea for a new type of conference, where teachers could play, create, explore, and collaborate, and they founded Playdate—People Learning and Asking Y: Digital Age Teacher Exploration (http://bit.ly/1C169wL). Along with some colleagues, they launched Playdate in Chicago in 2013, and ses-sions now span the globe as educators worldwide satisfy their need to col-laborate and play. (See Figure 2.2.)

Your Tribe

Whatever our passion, there is someone else out there who feels passion-ate about that topic as well. We just have to find that someone! Today, mil-lions of educators are looking to connect and collaborate. But connections don't just happen; we have to put ourselves out there, ask questions, and seek

Figure 2.2 Teachers Explore New Technology at a Playdate

professional relationships with those who will enhance our practice. As Mee-noo Rami says, find your people and your practice will thrive! Finding our tribe is building a community, in person and online, that nurtures our teaching soul and inspires us to be great. We can assemble tribes at our school, in our hometown, on social media, and at conferences.

Katie began building a tribe when she started following the *Two Writing Teachers* blog (http://bit.ly/1GP5AZK). For the first time she connected with educators online, sharing her professional practice with teachers outside her school. It also opened her eyes to online learning as a means to improve her classroom practice. Sold on the world of online interactions, she signed up for Twitter and started attending Edcamps, making connections with educators everywhere in the world. Katie introduces her students to global communities as well, demonstrating firsthand how building connections enriches a conversation and exposes us to new viewpoints. She now leans on her tribe for ideas, feedback, and some good old-fashioned laughs. Because, let's face it, teaching is a hard job.

Shortly after joining Twitter, Kristin found the #1stchat community, a group of worldwide first-grade teachers who meet online every Sunday at 8 p.m. eastern standard time to discuss first-grade curriculum, practices, and students. Making these connections has changed how Kristin plans her instruction. Instead of reading a journal article or searching for hours online to find the best book for a unit of study, Kristin now tweets or messages her #1stchat colleagues for feedback that has been teacher tested and kid approved. With the help of teachers who have already evaluated a resource or taught a lesson, Kristin ensures that her students' experiences are of the highest quality.

There are Twitter chats for just about any topic or community that you might want to join. (For more on Twitter for educators, check out Heinemann's free course at http://bit.ly/1f5e9rt.) The Twitter chats listed in Figure 2.3 will get you started. For a more comprehensive list of hashtags and chat times, visit http://bit.ly/1x3luPT.

#21stedchat	#edtechchat
#engchat	#titletalk
#wonderchat	#ADEchat
#edchat	#satchat

Figure 2.3 Popular Twitter Hashtags for Educators

FILTERING INFORMATION AND FINDING WHAT'S RIGHT FOR YOU

When we first began to explore technology, we were overwhelmed, to be honest. There are so many tools and products out there; how can a classroom teacher determine which ones are best for her students? As we mentioned earlier, we want to make sure that we are grounding our technology use in principles of good teaching. But that doesn't mean that we can't accept new tools, strategies, and ideas into our repertoire. We use research, exploration, and collaboration to ensure that the tools we discover will be useful and beneficial to us and our students.

Learn from Others' Experience

Watching another teacher in the classroom is powerful. Something within us is unlocked when we see how someone has planned, organized, and implemented a lesson. We might visit a teacher in our school or plan a visit to a nearby school whose use of technology we admire. We can also watch video clips online and purchase books and DVDs that show practice in action. The websites of the professional organizations mentioned earlier in the chapter provide a wealth of information and support materials. If we aren't able to see a lesson in action, talking with colleagues about what they've used, why, and how it worked for them is helpful, as is interacting on teacher blogs.

Find an Epicenter Practitioner

In *Reading in the Wild*, Donalyn Miller and Susan Kelley (2013) coin the term *epicenter reader* and talk about the importance of finding these readers in our personal life and in our classroom. Epicenter readers are the center points of change, the catalysts for elevating the reading lives of others by the sheer force of their passion and their ability to share that passion. We need to find epicenter technology users too—practitioners we respect and admire, people who are more connected than we ever may be and who are able to prefilter information and share the best of the best that's out there. They may teach a similar age group, approach technology in the classroom in a way we connect with, or challenge how we view the world. We find epicenter technology users across the hall, across the state, or across the world. Technology connects us in ways never possible before and helps us develop our passion and practice.

We are lucky enough to have many epicenter technology users right down the hall (a by-product of growing meaningful technology practices school-wide). But many of our PLN gurus have a strong online presence and are followed by teachers around the world. Our list grows every day, just as our tribe increases with each new Twitter chat and Edcamp. Here are just a few of our epicenter technology users you might find helpful as you begin your journey.

Jennie Magiera, www.teachinglikeits2999.com

A colleague of ours in Chicago, Jennie Magiera is a leader in educational technology, and her fast-paced presentations are filled with tidbits and truths that leave her audience feeling inspired about the possibilities to empower students. From app reviews to face-to-face meetings with developers and decision makers, Jennie puts her kids in the driver's seat and lets them show why these tools matter.

Steven Anderson, http://blog.web20classroom.org

Based in North Carolina, educator and blogger Steven Anderson inspires us daily with ideas to use in our classrooms. His understanding of how to use social media with students, mixed with clear expectations and pedagogy, makes his blog a great place to search out innovative tools, lessons, and ideas.

Silvia Rosenthal Tolisano, http://langwitches.org/blog

Silvia Tolisano currently resides in Brazil, but that doesn't stop her from effecting change in classrooms around the world. Her website and blog offer practical ideas and promote the use of technology as a means to connect students to the wider world and develop global perspectives on education. We love Silvia's work; it inspires us to get connected with and learn from educators worldwide.

Richard Byrne, www.freetech4teachers.com

Richard Byrne gives us a daily dose of educational technology from the high school perspective. He shows how practices we begin and support are continued in high school. Richard's passionate and thoughtful site focuses on practical tips that any teacher can use in his or her classroom.

Luis Perez, http://luisperezonline.com

Luis is an inclusive learning specialist and our go-to resource for thinking about *all* our students' specific needs with regard to technology in the classroom. His site offers tips and tricks for using technology to transform learning for all students, whatever their needs.

Start with What You Have

Sometimes we don't have a choice in the tools, programs, or apps we're provided; we have to do the best we can with what we have. It may also be the case that you have devices but it feels like a labor of love (or sometimes hate) to get them going. Complicated checkout systems and schedules, dated devices that take twenty minutes to boot, and dodgy Internet connections make us want to throw in the towel. A few years ago Katie's primary desktop computer could be turned on only by sticking a paper clip in the side! It's a wonder she wasn't electrocuted. But roadblocks are a normal part of this digital world we live in.

The best way to navigate this often bumpy road is to become an advocate for what students need. If your kids need iPads so they can archive their learning, make it known. If you need your students to connect with the world through a blog, make a pitch to your principal or superintendent and show examples of classrooms that are connecting with other classrooms in a powerful way. Teachers in Chicago advocated for YouTube and Twitter in the classroom by demonstrating how they would be used for learning; both tools are now available to enhance instruction.

Focus on What You Can Do and Enlist Help

A good place to start is with what you can do, not what you can't do. Focusing on what we don't have, what doesn't work, or what we think our students can't do creates an atmosphere where challenges inhibit learning and students are unable to grow.

We have to focus on what we or our students can do at this moment and use that as a starting point for our work. If we can say to ourselves, "I can learn," we're more than halfway there.

We need to take a can-do attitude and either find others who feel the same way or convince people to join us. We seek out colleagues in our building who also want to move forward with technology. We try things out and invite our administrators to join us. Build your tribe with the tools we mentioned so you don't feel isolated in your journey.

We are not experts in all things technology. We know what we know and we always strive to learn more. But when trouble arises, whether it be issues with devices or deep questions about the relevance and importance of the new practices we employ, we turn to our tribe to get us through.

CONNECTING TECH TO YOUR STUDENTS

Logan bent over his desk, intent on his work, blocking out the noise of the students working around him. This wasn't the first time Katie had seen him sitting hunched in his chair. He was usually stationed at his desk, nose in a book or eyes on the ceiling. Logan was polite and well-mannered, but he didn't often talk to his peers, and when he did, it frequently ended in an argument.

Today was different. He was deeply engaged in designing a game using a simple coding application Katie had found the previous weekend. (Although she'd made sure the app was appropriate, she didn't know how to create the game. The students needed to read, explore, and discover how to do it themselves.)

This time Logan talked himself through his frustrations instead of stopping. Carmela, his table neighbor, asked what he was doing. "I'm designing a game," he responded proudly.

"Whoa! That's so cool! Can I play it?" Carmela asked. Logan beamed as he showed her how to get started. Soon other students were begging for a turn. Logan stood proudly at the center of the group and explained his work, the plans for his design, how the codes worked, and the challenges he'd faced. He saw he had things in common with classmates; his passion for gaming became an entry point into a community where he had previously struggled to find connection.

Unleash the Power of Play

Play is collaborative, experiential, tactile, and active (Carroll 2013). When children play, they are preparing themselves to become a part of society, exploring roles that adults fill in daily life. Play has been shown to maintain (and potentially grow) flexible neural connections within our brains and has been linked to building skills related to critical thinking, communication, problem solving, and collaboration (Marano 1999). According to Randa Grob-Zachary, CEO of the LEGO Foundation, play fosters creativity and sparks intellectual curiosity.

"Learning by doing deepens our engagement and understanding significantly, and strengthens the most important pathways our brains use to learn and develop" (Kanani 2014). Play is not a luxury; it's a way to support brain development in our students, and it reconnects us with the joy of discovery we had as children. Research shows that "play-based learning with playful teachers heightens overall long term academic performance" (Golinkoff and Hirsch-Pasek 2014). Through play we discover new possibilities, build relationships, and think in divergent pathways—three essential ingredients in opening our practice to new tools for learning.

Once we hear about a tool, see it being used, and bring it into our classroom, playing with it is how we find out how it works, what it can do, and why we should use it with our students. We determine which things we will need to explicitly teach and model for students to get them started and which things they can discover as they work independently. It's not about this one tool today but rather the process of discovery and learning. The devices and apps available as we write this book will be different or gone in a matter of years, maybe sooner. Tried-and-true tools and apps get updates that change everything with the click of a button. Play is essential for keeping up with the fast pace of technology. Here are four ways to inspire play in your classroom.

- *Infuse play into the daily routine.* Children want to play. Anyone who has been zapped in the head with a rubber band from a geoboard knows that even well-meaning students have a strong desire to play with anything new and different. Capitalize on this desire by making your classroom a joyful, playful place in which children learn and have fun! Provide learning experiences that encourage creativity, experimentation, and expression. When introducing a new tool, invite students to explore it for a few minutes and share what they've learned. Provide ample time for students to turn and talk so they can process their learning and share ideas. Encourage students to create and interpret drawings, photos, and infographics, and use this time as an opportunity to teach media literacy. Most important, allocate time for all students to create their own messages and content; doing so is naturally engaging and motivating.

- *Offer a variety of tools and experiences.* Play doesn't have to start with technology. We invite students to explore and play by manipulating items, examining lifelike models, wondering about the world around them, and creating with a variety of tools. Technology can build on that play time by opening students to possibilities like moviemaking, coding, robotics, and other forms of twenty-first-century play. We also encourage students to combine ideas, talents, and media to invent new ways to use items and new purposes for the tools they have at hand.

- *Use play to build community.* Play can also be a powerful community-building tool as students work in teams to collaborate, solve problems, and develop communication skills. At the beginning of each year, Katie has her students participate in the Marshmallow Challenge (http://bit .ly/1Te4v5B). Student teams use collaborative creative thinking to build the tallest freestanding structure they can out of twenty sticks of spaghetti, one yard of tape, one yard of string, and one marshmallow, which must rest on top. (See Figure 2.4.) This friendly competition goes beyond an icebreaker activity as students work together to plan and design their towers.

Figure 2.4 Students Work on the Marshmallow Challenge

- *Encourage divergent thinking.* Instead of focusing on what a tool was created to do, encourage students to explore new uses. Model how you layer apps to work together, invite students to make stop-motion films, allow kids to compose with music-creation apps, then push them to think about how those tools might be used in different ways. Providing students a real audience and connecting them with learners and specialists around the world can spur them to think differently. As you help students understand and refine their knowledge of technology, notice and note how they use applications in combination or reach an audience with a new message. Invite students to share their innovative thinking with the class. Ultimately, you want them to push the envelope on what can be done using the tools at their disposal. (See Figure 2.5.)

Figure 2.5 Students Project a Drawing of a Skyline onto Their Block City

Determine What Your Students Can Do with This Technology

When selecting tools for your classroom, look for those that invite students to create, collaborate, and connect. There's a lot of clutter out there: you don't need sixty-seven applications for digital publishing. Find a few tools that kids can use diversely—to draw, publish, record. Then invite kids to find new opportunities to use these tools. A learning management system (LMS) like Edmodo or Schoology lets students, in large or small groups, share work with one another and you, have collaborative discussions, and manage their work. A drawing app can be used to prepare visualizations for a read-aloud, craft original artwork, or annotate an image. A movie-creation tool might be used to make book trailers or document a child's process or a scientific experiment. We want to choose tools that provide students with infinite opportunities to create, interact, and connect.

Determine How Easy It Is for Your Students to Use

Although we shouldn't automatically disqualify a tool for being complicated, it's important to think about the practicality of launching a tool and the amount of time it will take to teach students to use it. Something that might seem complicated at first glance can often be easy to use after you've learned how to operate it. However, a tool that's consistently difficult to use, either because the controls aren't intuitive or because it's poorly designed, is a no go. Classroom time is too precious to waste.

Just as we wouldn't let students abandon writing memoirs on the first day of a unit, we also shouldn't give up on a technology tool before we get to know it. Give the tool a fair and thorough exploratory period before discounting it. If you encounter issues, reach out to other users for solutions. Start with tools that others recommend and build from there. Technology is a fine balance of time spent versus payoff; seek tools that maximize instructional time and guide students to independence.

Determine How Students Will Be Able to Share Their Work

If we want students to create meaningful products, not just consume information, they have to be able to share their work easily. Can they email from the app? Can they post their work to their blog? Can they upload it to another location? Will students be able to share their work independently or will we need to help them?

If students are unable to share work independently, the job falls to you. It can be difficult to upload thirty book trailers to the classroom Vimeo account, so you may need to make plans to enlist the help of parent volunteers or assistants or choose a tool students can manage themselves. Blocked websites and slow Internet connections sometimes affect the size of files students can share. It's always best to test the steps beforehand so you know what you need to teach students in order for them to share successfully. Your district's policy on how students share and access work is also a consideration. All of this requires conversations with colleagues and with district administrators advocating for what students need in order to be able to share, connect, and create for the world. Figure 2.6 lists some questions to ask when evaluating apps.

Reflect and Envision

We can look at technological tools in two ways. On one side you have reflection. This is where you look at your classroom practice and determine a need that you might address with technology. These needs arise from our students, either as a group or as individuals. Perhaps students need a way to share their work

* What can my students do with this app? What creative capabilities does it have?
* How much time will it take for students to learn to use it?
* In what ways can students share their work from the app?
* What teacher-friendly controls or features does it offer?
* Are there any privacy or security concerns?
* What can this app do that none of the other classroom apps do?
* How will this enhance or enrich what I'm already doing?

Figure 2.6 Questions to Ask When Evaluating Apps

more fluidly. Perhaps a group of students is struggling to access curriculum. Approaching technology this way, we have a clear idea of what we need and what we want. We set everything else aside or put it on hold while we search for just the right tool.

The other side of the coin is discovering something we never considered or thought possible. We might read a blog post about using blogging with students and see it as a valuable tool for getting our students to articulate and share how they solve math problems. Perhaps we discover the back-channel tool TodaysMeet at a conference and realize it is an effective way to engage all our learners in a discussion. When we envision what's possible, we're open to learning and exploring new tools and ideas. We examine these tools with careful eyes and an open mind, while still thinking about how this new idea or tool will enhance the good practices we've established in our classroom, and we look for opportunities to extend, expand, and enhance our teaching and our students' learning.

Three Things to Try Tomorrow

Set Aside Thirty Minutes a Week to Discover and Play

To accomplish something, you have to make time for it. Set aside thirty minutes a week in which to reach out to your tribe for new ideas and/or play with new tools or new ways to use tools. Catch up on your favorite blogs, check out a Twitter chat, comb through a favorite website, or explore a new tool, all the while thinking, *What if?* This might be an individual endeavor, something you do early Saturday morning before the house wakes up, fresh coffee in hand. Or perhaps you and a few colleagues meet at lunch once a week to read, chat, share, and play. Choose a time that works for you and that you can stick to. If you can't find time to meet with colleagues but would like to share ideas, set up a Google Doc for everyone to access and type in a few notes or links each week. Each teacher can add or share their thinking at any time, so it's a great way to keep track of all of your explorations and ideas.

Carve Out Classroom Time for Students to Discover and Play

You need to create time for your students to explore as well: twenty minutes every Wednesday or five minutes just before lunch every day. Students need to explore the tools you have in order to build their familiarity with what's possible, gain independence, and get their creative juices flowing. Establish the expectation that when they discover something that may be valuable to the class, they share. Students will soon become visionaries, eager to offer a discovery, a tip, or a trick. This isn't free time when students play games on a device, but exploration time, when they play and explore with the intention of discovering something new or finding a new way of doing something they can share with the class.

Sign Up for a Conference, Webinar, or Edcamp

We do better in groups, and teaching is a vast road to travel alone. Connect! Find a conference, webinar, or Edcamp that you can sign up for in the next six months. Don't wait; do it now. Edcamps are popping up all over the country (and the world); you can usually find one that's close to home and free. Webinars, like the ones Heinemann offers, are great because you can learn in the comfort of your own home. Conferences expose you to a wide range of ideas and provide opportunities to network with colleagues and make new ed tech friends. If your district or PTA can help fund your learning, great, but don't let footing the bill yourself hold you back. If we wait for someone to pay for our learning opportunities, we may never get any.

 Scan this QR code or visit http://hein.pub/amplify to see videos of teachers and students in action and access up-to-date resources for this book (use keycode AMPLIFY15).

3
CHAPTER

Connecting Technology to Existing Classroom Practice

What does it look like when we merge new technologies with our existing classroom practice? What can it look like? And what are we able to do now that we couldn't do before?

Kristin's first graders sit snuggled on the classroom carpet, listening to her read a picture book aloud. They use an iPad drawing app to capture their thinking as she reads, stopping periodically to share their work with a partner. These young learners are developing writers and this digital boost helps them articulate their thinking and share it with a wider audience, and it gives Kristin more information about each child as a learner.

She asks them to choose three annotations that showcase their thinking about the book and add them to a slideshow created on SonicPics, an app that allows them to enhance images with audio recordings and captions. Although they've used this tool before, Kristin models the process on her own iPad, reinforcing the necessary skills: "Friends, you're going to add audio to your images or words so that viewers hear more about your thinking. Watch as I show you how to do this." She adds audio to her images, describing each step aloud. Kids then scatter around the room with their iPads and head-phones and start to record.

Kristin listens in as the students work. Grace is recording her thinking about her first image: "One new thing I learned was that you need to wear spikes to climb Mount Everest." She swipes the screen to move to the next drawing in her slideshow. "I also learned that 107 people have died trying to climb it." She moves on to the final image. "But one thing I was wondering was how do the Sherpas learn how to climb?" She then reviews her video clip before exporting it as a movie file. Grace has accomplished the goals of the lesson: summarizing new learning and questions from the read-aloud by elaborating on her drawings.

Jackson stumbles over his words halfway through. He brings his iPad to Kristin and asks if there's a way he can start over. Kristin shows him how to go back and rerecord his thoughts and asks him to be the classroom rerecording specialist. She then sends a few students who approach her with the same problem to Jackson.

To conclude the lesson, Kristin calls students back to the rug for a debriefing. Kristin collaborates with students to capture the steps they used on an anchor chart they can refer to in the future (see Figure 3.1).

Having students annotate their thinking during read-alouds makes their thinking visible and helps learning stick. Either on paper or digitally, children capture their new learning and questions, and we use these responses to plan follow-up lessons for small-group instruction and conferences. Digital tools enhance this process by offering the potential to share and archive work in multiple ways.

Headphones with built-in microphones help preserve recording quality in crowded classrooms. We asked for donations, wrote grants for them, and eventually added them to our school supply lists.

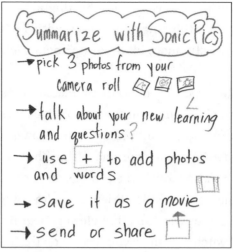

Figure 3.1 Anchor Chart for Summarizing with SonicPics

Once we've discovered tools to try, it can feel daunting to connect them to our existing classroom practice. Where do we start? How will it look? How is the technology better, different, or more involved than what we were already doing? These are all good questions. We're not going to tell you to jump in and everything will be fine. It might be fine, it might be mind-blowing, or it might fall flat. Change is hard, and occasional flops are to be expected. But there are some ways to ensure that we're connecting these new ideas and tools to solid practices that have been proven to make a difference in student learning.

CONTINUE TO GIVE STUDENTS OPPORTUNITIES TO READ, WRITE, AND TALK

In 2013, we saw Donalyn Miller, author of *The Book Whisperer* (2009), present at the annual National Council of Teachers of English conference and were struck by one phrase in particular: "The only thing kids need to be doing during reading workshop is reading books, talking about books, and writing about books." That sounds simple, but if we look carefully at our classroom strategies, we may find what Donalyn calls "language arts and crafts"—projects without educational value that don't help children become better readers and that ultimately end up wasting precious time. It happens to all of us. The danger of technology falling into this category is strong.

We need to teach kids to think and read strategically, be aware of their own thinking, and recognize the power in that thinking. Reading, writing about reading, and talking about reading are the tools we use to get students there (Harvey and Goudvis 2013). To become successful readers, students need explicit modeling and guidance on when and how to best use a strategy and varied levels of collaborative practice that ultimately result in independent practice and mastery (Pearson and Dole 1987). Using technology as part of collaborative practice adds layers of support. Figure 3.2 lists some technology-infused experiences that can authentically enhance curriculum.

Balance Digital Text with Printed Text

Sometimes it's difficult for students to read a text on a digital device and respond on that same device. Although some students can easily navigate between two or more open platforms on a computer, many cannot, especially those who are still mastering the art of reading. We want technology to help students, not hinder them. Reading an article on the *Time for Kids* website and posting comments about it on Edmodo at the same time isn't user-friendly; it slows learners down and impedes the deep thinking reading requires. We use

Reading	Writing	Talking
• Read an article on a current events website. • Explore infographics. • View images or media related to a current unit of study. • Access challenging texts via a multitouch book (audio, weblinks, and video embedded for support) or an audiobook.	• Respond on a classroom blog to something one has recently read or learned. • Have a small-group digital discussion, or "silent dialogue." • Take a photo of the cover of a book one is reading independently and annotate it with thinking about the book. • Experiment with digital organizational tools or graphic organizers.	• Record a short reflection of lingering questions or reactions. • Record a "talking head" response and share it with the class. • Reflect on a new technology tool in a face-to-face discussion. • Pair discussion and digital tools to maximize engagement.

Figure 3.2 Reading, Writing, and Talking Through Technology

work-arounds in these situations, sometimes using a tool like dotEPUB to pull the text of a website article into a format where students *can* highlight and jot notes on their device easily. If this option isn't available, we ask them to use paper and pencil to capture their thinking.

Sometimes we feel that when we want to *really* read something, we need to see it on paper. Digital text does affect the physical act of reading: the clarity of the words on the screen, the presence of hyperlinks, and how quickly one can navigate the material impact the reading experience. Although researchers are still trying to determine the long-term effects of reading digital text, one thing is clear: good print reading doesn't automatically translate to successful digital reading. Because digital reading requires a different set of skills, we must explicitly teach students how to attack digital text strategically (Konnikova 2014).

> There are many great interactive sites and applications you might use that invite students to draw, write, doodle, respond, and capture thinking while they read or research—Popplet, Explain Everything, Educreations, and Linoit.com are a few of our favorite tools.

We need to be intentional about how we present texts to our students and how we have them respond. Variety is the spice of life. To keep kids engaged, we need to expose them to a wide range of tools and uses, mix up groupings and configurations, and diversify our teaching strategies. Here's what a typical week might look like:

Monday: Read aloud the first part of an article, modeling your thinking. Students, in pairs, finish reading the article on paper, jotting down their thinking. Each student then posts an individual response on a Padlet wall. At the end of the workshop, students look at the Padlet wall together and discuss common themes in their responses.

Tuesday: Students select an article from one of the approved classroom reading websites, read it online, and take notes in their notebook under the headings "What I Learned" and "What I Wonder." At the end of workshop, small groups share what they learned and any lingering questions they have.

Wednesday: The class reads aloud the wonder of the day on Wonderopolis. Students turn and talk about the content, post their wonderings on a class anchor chart, and possibly leave a comment on the website. (Students periodically follow up on their wonderings to research and find answers.)

Thursday: Load classroom devices with PDF copies of digital texts. During reading workshop every student chooses and reads one of the articles, annotates it using a PDF annotator, and emails you his or her work for assessment.

Friday: Read aloud a picture book, modeling your thinking. Pause occasionally for students to turn and talk. When you're finished, ask students to jot down the reading strategies they saw you use and record a one-minute video reflection summarizing their thinking.

Balance and diversity make the week's instruction full of experiences to read, write, and talk about text. Students work in various configurations—as a class, with a partner, in small groups, and individually. Prioritizing student response keeps kids deeply engaged.

Model and Practice Online Reading and Research

Modeling is essential to online reading. Julie Coiro (2011) concludes that in order for students to become successful online readers, they must be explicitly taught how to read online texts. She suggests that reading text punctuated with links leads to weaker comprehension and cites the well-known study (Nielsen 2006) identifying how adult readers read digital texts—skimming and scanning down the page in an F pattern, viewing and decoding fewer words as they go. We find this study concerning, but it offers imperative feedback for how we should approach digital reading instruction with our students. We wonder whether the F-pattern reading style is a response to not being taught explicitly how to read a digital text online. While we know it will take years of research to obtain the answer to this question, our classroom practices have shown that providing explicit modeling, naming strategies proficient readers use, and identifying the potentials for distraction in online text guide our students to become more skilled readers of digital text.

One day Katie asked her fifth graders to read and respond to a website article several pages long and was surprised when they began buzzing and chatting within minutes. They had read only the first page, not understanding they needed to click the arrow at the bottom of the web page to continue reading the following pages. Katie presented an impromptu minilesson on how to progress through a digital text, modeling how to read the page and follow the hyperlinks to the end. Naming a feature encountered while reading digitally and providing explicit instruction on how to navigate it gives students the starting points they need to read and comprehend text on this new platform.

We need to acquaint our students with digital features that can sidetrack them when they are reading online (Harvey et al. 2013). Stephanie Harvey and her coauthors ask that we teach kids to be "thinking intensive learners," encouraging the mindset that reading is thinking, that the questions we ask and address matter, and that it's not always about finding answers but about continuing to seek new knowledge. Figure 3.3 lists some possible minilessons.

Noticing Web Features
- Ask students to observe features of websites that both help and distract them.
- Create a class chart of helpful features and what they do or mean.
- Identify strategies that will help students deal with distractions.

Evaluating Internet Sources
- With your students, evaluate a variety of websites.
- Share both credible and noncredible websites and ask students to determine which are which.
- Create a chart of suggestions to help students evaluate Web resources independently.

Evaluating Infographics
- With your students, read and interpret a selection of infographics.
- Have students notice elements, ask questions, and attempt to determine what the author is trying to accomplish.
- Help students determine whether the author and information may be biased.

Annotating Thinking Digitally
- On a T-chart, list ways to document new learning and questions when reading online versus reading print.
- Ask students to view a short video and respond using a drawing tool.
- Take a photo of a piece of text and use a drawing tool to annotate the photo.

Reading Media
- View a selection of media clips and discuss how bias or stereotypes may distract from the message.
- Investigate online images for alteration or exaggeration.

Figure 3.3 Minilessons That Help Kids Read Online   *(adapted from Harvey et al. 2013)*

PROVIDE ACCESS AND OWNERSHIP
FOR ALL STUDENTS

We want all students to participate and learn—not 50 percent or 80 percent or even 90 percent, but every kid, every day, all year long. When kids are invested in their learning, when they have a say in guiding the curriculum, *they* are doing the work.

In many schools when the bell rings at the end of the day, students burst out the doors ready to attend a club, go to basketball practice, or engage in any number of similar extracurricular activities. They're energized and full of excitement. When their teachers finally leave the building, they come out sweating, hair askew, exhausted. How is it students end the school day with so much more energy? Smokey Daniels would say it is because their teachers are doing all the work. Too often we plan the "perfect lesson" and put on a show for our kids, unintentionally robbing them of what they need most—time to do the work. Stephanie Harvey likes to say, "The one who does the most work learns the most!" We must make sure our students are the ones who question, investigate, converse, and produce in order to build knowledge that matters to them. Our role is to serve as the guide on the side, to facilitate their becoming happy, healthy, productive members of society.

All children can learn. We have countless opportunities each day to invite kids to do the work and build understanding. Leveraging technology is one way to make that happen. Technology gives kids access and amplifies opportunities for interaction. In a digital conversation, every student participates; no one is left out. The anonymity of the typed text levels the field, providing support for those who struggle to access the curriculum.

Educator, researcher, and author Alan November (2012) asks some important questions: "Are your students leaving a legacy? How are they contributing to the world? How are they creating content and helping other people learn?" His framework establishes an authentic purpose for work that students set for themselves. Kids who are challenged to look at all the tools they have at their disposal to solve problems and make change in the world own their learning.

Use Visual Media

Images and video clips are powerful classroom tools. They can be used to build background knowledge, prompt meaningful questions, and develop inference skills. Not too long ago Kristin scoured bookstores during the summer, purchasing discount calendars for the quality images. She used these detailed, high-quality photos to develop her students' thinking strategies. Today, we can find beautiful images related to curriculum or students' interests at the click of a button.

Whatever their reading level, all students can study an image and think deeply about it. And all kids need explicit instruction on how to view to learn. Technology has made images and media clips a part of daily life. The first thing we see when we open a news website is an image or a video. Sports apps are loaded with infographics. Even our newspapers are becoming image heavy. We no longer define reading only as decoding and comprehending text; we now teach kids to read images, artifacts, and short video clips. In *Falling in Love with Close Reading* (2014), Chris Lehman and Kate Roberts advocate teaching kids to read text, media, and life. By reading, viewing, and studying something closely, we "model for students that their lives are rich with significance, ready to be examined, reflected upon and appreciated" (2). Each moment of life we "read," we immerse kids in intensive thinking. We teach them how to analyze and evaluate, make inferences, identify bias, critique, and comprehend multimedia.

We need to introduce our students to these new formats and explicitly teach how to interact with and navigate them. We must use layered texts and reimagine the definition of reading to embrace all forms of media literacy. The Transliteracy Research Group defines transliteracy as "the ability to read, write, and interact across a range of platforms, tools, and media from signing and orality through handwriting, print, TV, radio, and film to digital social networks" (Newman 2010). So how do we teach kids to think about images and media—to wonder, infer, assess their validity, identify bias and motive, and build an understanding of how images can communicate a message?

Begin a Unit of Study with Images

Having students study digital images related to a curricular inquiry develops the background knowledge necessary for the new investigation and helps them understand the unit as it unfolds. It's also a great way to build excitement for future learning! You might ask them to select three or four images they wonder about, add these images to a podcast or movie, and record themselves asking questions about them. These short movies tell you what students know and want to know before the inquiry begins, and you can personalize your instruction based on this information. At the end of the unit students can use these movies for self-assessment: did they find the answers to their questions? Having done so is clear evidence of learning. Not having done so is an opportunity to explore lingering questions and undertake further research.

Pair Media with Text

Pairing images or media clips with text helps students build background knowledge and access new learning; it also lets them practice synthesizing information. Short videos are opportunities to layer viewing, listening, writing, speaking, and responding into a lesson. For example, on Wednesdays, we often watch the short video clip that the website Wonderopolis pairs with the text announcing the wonder of the day. These two- to four-minute videos are the perfect length for kids to practice viewing to learn. We explicitly teach them to watch with a wide-awake mind by noting and naming the differences between viewing for enjoyment and viewing to learn new information. Students jot down thinking and observations on a sticky note, a two-column chart, or a digital collaboration tool.

Use Digital Tools to Include All Learners

Over the years we've come to understand the value of engaging students verbally. We give kids opportunities to share their thinking, hear the thinking of others, and process information in small groups and pairs. We teach conversation and collaboration skills explicitly and help students understand and practice the nuances of group conversation, including body language. These are essential skills we never want to sacrifice.

How many students are able to respond or contribute in a typical whole-class conversation? A classroom discussion board or a collaborative document or app ensures that every student makes a contribution and every student in the class benefits from all the rich thinking and learning that is taking place. It's a way for all students to share their thinking without waiting for a turn; sometimes when kids wait, they are so focused on what they want to say that they forget to listen to the amazing ideas being shared. Digital tools provide new and different ways for students to interact. They might do any of the following:

- react to and discuss a read-aloud, short story, poem, or nonfiction article
- discuss observations and results of a small-group science experiment and compare results with those of other small groups
- analyze a piece of writing to tease out effective qualities of the genre
- debate a current events issue
- ask questions or share new learning

Digital conversations offer the added benefit of allowing us to examine all students' contributions and assess the depth of their understanding, their ability to respond to and build on their classmates' thinking, and how often they participate. We still value face-to-face conversations with kids and listening in as they chat with one another, but this additional layer of information helps us be more thorough.

Every classroom discussion, every digital interaction, is an opportunity to help children take their first steps into the global community, to see and define how, why, and when technology can be a vehicle of change. This increased interconnectivity sets the stage for students to develop deep compassion for one another and be upstanders in their community and the world. This is empowerment at its very core. Kids can own their learning, and technology is just one tool to get us there.

Differentiate Instruction

Accepting ownership of technology will be more challenging for some students than others. But that's OK. We're here to support them in their efforts and address their varied needs. Sometimes we can anticipate which students may struggle; other times they surprise us. Some students write short when they need to write long or long when they need to write short. They respond too quickly or not quickly enough. Digital communication is a skill, and our students need support, guidelines, and modeling to master it. Here are some suggestions for differentiating instruction to meet students' needs:

- *Make groups small.* In the intermediate grades, digital conversations work best with no more than five students in a group, so they are able to follow one another's comments, respond, build on thinking, and ask clarifying questions. In larger groups where students are proficient writers the conversations may move too quickly and students may become frustrated and lost.

- *Establish shared expectations for participation.* Be clear about expectations. A back-and-forth conversation may consist of a sentence or a short paragraph. A comment on a blog is usually a few sentences but might be longer. A reflection post or summary of thinking can be a paragraph to several paragraphs. You don't want to be too specific, but many students will spend too little or too much time without guidelines.

- *Experiment with student groupings.* Consider grouping students by technological ability, not academic ability. Group students flexibly and fluidly—occasionally allow the pokey puppies and rapid rabbits to work together. Kids need to work with a wide variety of students, and teamwork and collaboration are necessary life skills. However, sometimes it's appropriate to place students with a slower digital pace—those who like to read slowly and respond thoughtfully or who are still developing their typing skills—in the same group.

- *Provide scaffolds and support.* Struggling students need to engage with their classmates and we need to help them do so. Do they need access to materials ahead of time? Do they need help choosing words? Or is transcription appropriate? Preteach text or vocabulary, collaborate with special educators and bilingual teachers, provide sentence stems or other supports—any strategy is fair game.

BUILD A COMMUNITY OF LEARNERS

A frequent observation made by educators who visit our school is that students work so well together. This is not by accident and not because we've been blessed with nice kids. Our students treat one another well because we explicitly teach them to collaborate starting in the youngest grades. Community, both offline and online, is a school-wide priority. Community enables our students to get to know one another, develop trusting relationships, and take risks in the classroom.

Before we begin teaching our students about technology, we build a classroom community that is respectful, inclusive, and supportive. We've been influenced by Peter Johnston's *Choice Words* (2004), Stephanie Harvey and Harvey "Smokey" Daniels' *Comprehension and Collaboration* (2009), Debbie Miller's *Reading with Meaning* (2013), and many other books, blogs, TED Talks, and conferences. Following are our guiding principles:

- Include students in classroom decisions.
- Establish classroom guidelines.
- Model and encourage positive language.
- Use fluid and flexible groups.
- Be aware of and coach students who need assistance with the social aspect of learning.
- Take community online.

Establish Classroom Guidelines

By the end of the first week of school, we and our students cocreate classroom expectations for what they feel will support them in having a safe and caring learning environment. These aren't rules but rather procedures for how we do things, and they are incorporated into a compact (or constitution or credo) that guides all interactions within the classroom.

Early in the first week, Kristin reads aloud books that spur discussion of community, collaboration, and conflict resolution. These early read-alouds lay the foundation for how the students will treat one another and who they will become. From day one, Kristin notices and notes her students' actions ("Wow! That was so kind of you to hold the door open for Jose!") and language ("Friends, did you hear when Dylan just told Matthew that was a good question and he should write that down? That's the type of talk that signals smart thinking."). During the week she initiates conversations about classroom interactions that encourage collaboration, teamwork, kindness, effort, responsibility, and ownership. She invites students to add their ideas and examples to a classroom chart. On Friday she and the students have a class meeting in which they combine the behavior and skills of a positive classroom community into a classroom compact like the one in Figure 3.4, which each child signs. (Figure 3.5 is an example of an intermediate-grade class compact.) She posts it in a central location and sends copies home. This compact is central to all lessons, and by the end of the year it is surrounded by art, images, and student work demonstrating that this space and place belongs to all the learners in it.

Some tips for creating classroom guidelines:

- *Provide structure.* Structure helps children envision and generate ideas. Ask kids to identify what an ideal classroom looks like, sounds like, and feels like. An organizer with headings like "Words I Will Say," "Words I Would Like to Hear," "Emotions I Want to Feel," and "Support I'd Like to Receive" prompt kids to consider all aspects.

- *Accept all ideas.* When students are brainstorming, write everything down, even if you know it may not make it into the final compact. Students need to feel honored from day one. Later, help them edit and revise to capture the most important and essential ideas. When students say

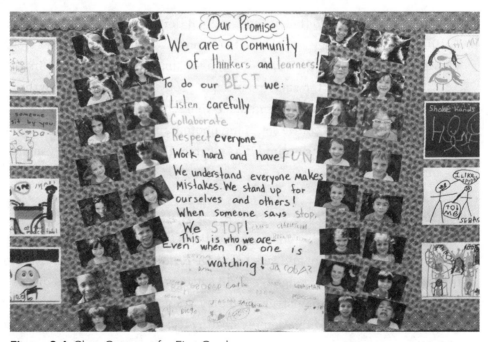

Figure 3.4 Class Compact for First Grade

Figure 3.5 Intermediate-Grade Class Compact

things like, "Listen to the teacher," write it down and prompt them to think about how they can also listen to one another.

- *Make it public.* Have each student sign the final compact. Hang it in a prominent place in the classroom. Send a copy home. Include it in the class blog. Refer to it often and make yourselves accountable for living up to the ideals you've set. Hang photographs or self-portraits of you and your students around it as a symbol of the community you are building together.

Model and Encourage Positive Language

How we talk with students and encourage them to talk to one another establishes the tone of the room and sets the stage for digital interactions. We expect students to use respectful language in all settings, from whole-class discussions to turn-and-talks to unstructured play. We don't just teach students skills; we build emotionally and relationally healthy learning communities (Johnston 2004). We move beyond language that values compliance ("I like the way you did that." or "Good job.") and use words that promote agency and build resiliency ("Tell me how you thought this through." or "What do you plan to do next?"). We guide students to listen actively so they can craft an appropriate response. We take these same ideas and phrases into our digital learning communities, giving students feedback that matters and modeling how to guide, discuss, and interact in any context.

Include Students in Classroom Decisions

Each year our teacher space gets smaller and smaller. We gave up our desks, moving our teacher stuff into a corner. We include lots of collaborative space, always getting thoughts, ideas, and feedback from the kids: there's only one of us and twenty-five to thirty of them. The idea that the space needs to work for everyone reinforces the community culture and honors students' voices in the classroom. Here are some ways our colleagues involve students in classroom decisions:

- Michelle Nash has her seventh graders help her research and select books for book clubs. Students who have choice and voice are more invested in doing the reading and participating in the discussions. She also allows groups to select how they will respond, offering a variety of options from sticky notes to digital collaboration.
- Eileen Bishop troubleshoots with her third graders once a week. They offer suggestions for dealing with disagreements or other issues that affect the classroom. Together they solve problems and are accountable for outcomes.
- Autumn Laidler invites her fourth graders to arrange the classroom furniture based on whether they will be working in pairs, with small groups, or as a whole class. Kids determine where to place their tables, chairs, and devices so they may collaborate most effectively.

Use Fluid and Flexible Groups

We ensure that everyone works with everyone. Each grouping brings a new learning dynamic; students benefit greatly from hearing fresh perspectives, having opportunities to practice conflict resolution skills, and getting to know one another better.

Be Aware of and Coach Students Who Need Assistance with the Social Aspect of Learning

There are students who need support in any community. Whether special needs affect their ability to socialize with peers or they just prefer not to, these students need understanding and guidance. Digital interactions often come much easier to these students, as the digital platform takes them out of the spotlight and invites them to work in a safe context alongside their classmates. But they may need accommodations, coaching, or other support in becoming comfortable and accepted within the classroom community.

Take Community Online

At some point, we move our face-to-face classroom community into the digital arena. Although the concept of digital citizenship goes beyond having respectful interactions with others online, this is a great place to start. Many of our minilessons regarding community have a digital community counterpart; see Figure 3.6. We also teach our students that tone and meaning can easily be misinterpreted in written discussions and comments because of the absence of body language.

Using technology helps build and enhance community. Technological tools are additional ways in which students can connect, interact, practice skills, and

Face-to-Face Community	Digital Community
• We use kind language when we talk to one another. We think about what we say before we say it. • We give one another specific feedback on things that worked well and gentle, constructive feedback on things that could be improved. • We use professional-sounding language and content-appropriate vocabulary. • We make an effort to connect with everyone, not just our friends.	• We use kind language when having digital discussions or leaving comments. We reread before we post to make sure we've said what we wanted to say. • We name specific parts of a post that we connect with. We suggest improvements carefully by saying, "I wonder if," or "I wish." • We use school-appropriate language—not too formal, not too casual. • We make an effort to connect with everyone, not just our friends.

Figure 3.6 Minilessons Promoting Face-to-Face and Digital Community

build relationships. Students discover mutual interests and recommend books via their blogs. They work on team projects. They build knowledge through shared discussion.

DEVELOP AN AUTHENTIC AUDIENCE FOR STUDENT WORK

We've long known that giving students an audience for their work is important and powerful. We communicate our thoughts and ideas as human beings in order to make an impact, have a voice, change the world. Interaction with an audience lets us know our work has been acknowledged and responded to. Yet so much of the writing, problem solving, and responding our students do is seen only by the teacher. Technology gives them access to a widespread audience and authentic reasons to write. That connection with audience then challenges us to rethink the types and quality of assignments we give students because it is not enough for us to set up blogs and have students do what they used to do in their notebooks.

Help Students Develop an Author's Voice and Connect with an Audience

To connect and empower students, we have to shift the balance of control. That may sound scary, but it doesn't mean turning the classroom over to the kids while we run out for coffee. It means turning over the ownership of the learning. We do this by using tools that help students feel the power and responsibility of ownership.

One of those tools is the individual student blog. They design the blog, are in charge of the content, and are responsible for anything they post. It's a place to publish written work, explain a challenging math problem, write about a topic of interest, or solicit feedback from their readers on a range of issues. Blogs honor authorship and provide a direct connection with audience.

We start our kids out as readers of blogs; to become proficient bloggers they need a vision for what they might craft. We introduce mentor blogs to help them get an idea of how to connect with their audience, structure their writing, and ultimately find their creative mojo. Figure 3.7 breaks down the process.

Primary Students	Intermediate Students
• Explain what blogs are, showing student blogs from previous years if possible. • Model writing an introductory blog, pointing out essential elements. • Create an anchor chart listing important reminders. • Have students write a collective class blog under your supervision. • When they are ready, have students start individual blogs by writing a "hello, world" post. • Have students share tips and tricks they learned while getting their blog posted. • Begin weaving blogging into various areas of the curriculum, coaching and encouraging students to try or do new things as the year goes on. • Emphasize that a blog is a two-way tool for communicating with real audiences.	• Get students excited by having them read and analyze a variety of mentor blogs. • Establish a focus for blogs. • Present minilessons on various formats, structures, ideas, and language conventions. • As the year goes on, encourage and coach students to try new blog styles or formats, experiment with video blogs, and embed images, links, and work created on apps. • Continually engage students in self-reflection through the lens of their audience. • Engage students in global blogging communities to build connections with other classrooms.

Figure 3.7 Launching Student Blogs

When we empower kids to be creative and share their ideas with a real audience, their projects take on a life of their own. A few years ago, fifth graders Merlin and Kiara wanted Katie to add a particular app to a class device. They claimed it was educational, so she asked them to find some official reviews to back up the claim. After exploring a variety of websites and blogs that featured app reviews, they were inspired to write their own reviews of apps they were using in school. They researched, planned, wrote, revised, and published their reviews on their own blogs. Their posts detailed how an app could be used to promote learning or capture thinking and provided examples of work created using the app. These early reviews inspired the entire class. The resulting flurry of app reviews caught the attention of lots of students and teachers (a few developers even asked the students for ideas on how to improve their apps). Talk about owning learning and affecting change with your words!

When we introduce blogs to students, we explicitly teach the nuances of both the technology and the medium: how to post, tag, and categorize; how to add images, links, and video; guidelines for proofreading and commenting (see Figure 3.8); and classroom expectations for reading and commenting on classmates' blogs (see Figure 3.9). Structured approaches include using a graphic organizer, sentence stems, or a theme to coach kids; once they become more proficient they can take the reins and experiment with language, format, and design. Kristin starts her young students off by having them introduce themselves to the world on their blog. She then connects blogging with Wonder Wednesdays. After exploring a wonder on the Wonderopolis site, students share their thoughts, their reactions, and their wonders. You might prefer to allow students to make their own path, coaching them individually through conferences and comments.

Expand Students' Audience Beyond the School Walls

Connecting to an audience gives kids an energizing boost! Audience starts with the classroom, then extends to families, the school community, peers around the world, authors, and experts. We teach kids how to respond to one another's

Figure 3.8 "What Does a Blog Comment Look Like and Sound Like?" Chart

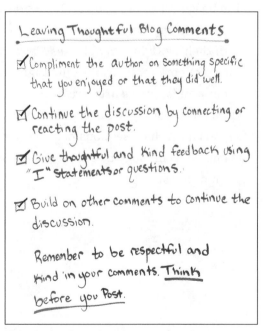

Figure 3.9 "Leaving Thoughtful Blog Comments" Chart

work as we model, suggest language, help them practice, and support them as they honor one another's accomplishments, set goals, and get feedback for improvement. Ultimately, we help them understand that our work together should be a celebration—not going around in a circle saying, "Good job," and "Nice post," but naming specific achievements, areas of growth, and things we connect with as readers and fellow learners. Occasionally we include families: invite them to a morning, afternoon, or evening event featuring student projects; send home business cards with student blog URLs; or email information on how to access our online work, along with suggestions for what kinds of comments are helpful.

Connecting your classroom to others in the school not only expands your students' audience but gives you the opportunity to brainstorm with a colleague. Would your fourth graders enjoy being blogging buddies with first graders? How might you connect classes beyond just leaving comments? Is there a shared topic, read-aloud, or strategy you could all be working on? Could third graders do a hands-on app demonstration for kindergartners? Would it be helpful for all sixth graders in the school to participate in a discussion or reflection? The possibilities are endless. It's a great recipe for effective collaboration.

Another approach might be to connect what students in your room are doing with their work in other classes. They can practice foreign language skills or share artwork on their blog, photograph a science experiment and then write about it in language arts, create a public service announcement advocating for more recess, or record themselves playing a musical piece and listen to how it sounds and which sections need more rehearsal. These opportunities allow you to embed technology meaningfully as part of the school day, not as a special event or a test.

Three Things to Try Tomorrow

Study an Image or a Video Clip

Find an image or a short video clip that you find perplexing, interesting, or inspirational—try the Digital Public Library of America (http://bit.ly/1f3Er8O); The Kid Should See This (http://bit.ly/1q3jhNJ); or, for older learners, the *New York Times* pictures of the day (http://nyti.ms/1QPhtTv). Gather your students and use this image or clip to spark a discussion. Let students linger with the image independently first and complete a graphic organizer with the headings "What I See" and "What I Think" (younger students can draw their thinking). If it's a short media clip, allow students to jot down their thinking, then show the clip again, pausing a few times for students to add additional comments and/or turn and talk.

Have a Digital Conversation

Select an article for students to read. Have them annotate it with their thinking as they go. Start with an easy tool like TodaysMeet (http://todaysmeet.com) and set up a "room" in which your students can discuss the article. Either give them a question to get started or have them contribute their own thoughts, reactions, and questions. Monitor and participate in the discussion as a co-learner, helping and coaching students as necessary.

Create a Classroom Compact

Start with a face-to-face community compact and then follow up with an online community compact. Have students turn and talk or jot down notes about the optimum environment for learning. Using student language, cowrite guidelines for student interactions online and offline that you will follow as a class. Model writing, revising, and rewriting the compact, either digitally or on chart paper.

 Scan this QR code or visit http://hein.pub/amplify to see videos of teachers and students in action and access up-to-date resources for this book (use keycode AMPLIFY15).

4

Foundational Lessons for Independence

Independence is a key skill that we encourage in all students. We want to foster an atmosphere where students use learning tools, including technology, autonomously. We set up systems and procedures for managing and using the tools, help students understand our expectations, and encourage them to be independent in their work. While these consistent structures take time, they are essential lessons in developing that independence that we seek for our students. In this chapter we describe eleven foundational lessons (see Figure 4.1) that set the

Developing Digital Citizens

Where Do We See Technology in Our Life?	Teach students to reflect on how and why we use technology in school and life.
Rights and Responsibilities	Students brainstorm a list of their rights and responsibilities as technology users.
Troubleshooting 101	Equip students with skills to solve problems independently.
Students as Specialists	Encourage students to step into specialist and teacher roles in the classroom.
Safeguarding Our Intellectual Property	Introduce kids to the idea of intellectual property.
The Priority Hierarchy	Teach students to organize and prioritize their time.

Managing Devices in the Classroom

The Care and Feeding of Technology Tools	Establish expectations for how to handle and care for devices when in use.
Classroom Signals	Establish a set of common signals to manage technology use in the classroom.
Surfing the Net	Establish guidelines for using the Internet in the classroom.
Naming and Sharing Work	Establish an organizational system for students' technology work.
What Looks the Same?	Help students apply what they already know about tools to new tools.

Figure 4.1 Foundational Lessons for Independence

stage for rich teaching and learning over the course of the year. They apply to all grade levels and devices and are separated into two categories: developing a mindset for becoming a digital citizen and establishing basic care and management procedures. You can teach these lessons as a unit at the beginning of the year or as the need arises. Adapt and adopt these lessons; make them your own. Teach and reteach them until they are second nature.

However and whenever you present these lessons, remember:

- *Link the tools to your classroom community values.* By doing so, you encourage students to use them confidently and reinforce the idea that community can be experienced digitally.
- *Emphasize tools that can be used for many purposes.* Kristin's first graders use drawing tools to track their thinking, respond to text, share mathematical processes, and more. Introducing these tools early on builds on a skill students are already familiar with, and Kristin can use them throughout the curriculum.
- *Create new anchor charts with students each year.* You may occasionally prepare sections ahead of time to prompt student thinking, but include students in the creation (and ultimately the ownership) of what goes up on the wall and why. For guidance on how to make anchor charts work for you, see *Smarter Charts*, by Marjorie Martinelli and Kristine Mraz (2012).

Where Do We See Technology in Our Life?

Technology impacts so much of our life today, both positively and negatively. Ask students to identify all the ways they see technology being used in the world and in their lives. Then show them the benefits of using technological tools in their schoolwork and point out potential distractions.

Why Teach This Lesson?

This early lesson opens a dialogue in which you and your students develop an understanding of how you want to use technology in your classroom. Establishing these expectations and norms together builds a healthy and respectful classroom community. It also acquaints you with students' technological background knowledge, experience, and access.

Lead-In

List all the ways you used technology to prepare for the school year and display it on chart paper, a document projector, or a digital device. Have students brainstorm ways they use or are impacted by technology and chart them together, as a starting point for discussing where they see technology having a role in the classroom.

Teach

"You came up with so many great ideas about where you see technology. What are you excited to do with technology this year? What have you been wanting to try out? Turn and talk with a partner for a minute and then we'll share our thinking as a class."

* * *

"I especially like Sadie's point that her mom uses her phone to buy coffee and that sometimes it doesn't work. That happens to me, too! Technology can be really helpful, but it can also slow things down if I don't know how to use something or if it's not working properly. What do you think about that as students? Are there times when we should maybe hold off on using technology in the classroom? How can we know if we should use technology or not?"

This lesson forces you to examine your own biases about technology. We've all had negative experiences, such as when our significant other or our children pulled out devices during dinner when we wanted to talk face-to-face. Students with a device in their hand will want to fidget with it as they might with a pencil, bit of paper, or notebook. Before assuming students aren't listening or are doing something they shouldn't, observe whether they really are listening and just keeping their hands busy. Set clear guidelines and teach students how to switch between listening and creating.

Remember and Reteach

Hang the chart that you created together somewhere you can refer to it in the coming days. It's the foundation for the remaining lessons and will help students envision a classroom in which technology is a tool for learning and creativity. You may need to reteach this lesson periodically. Students may choose to play on a device if given (or by making!) an opportunity. Keeping technology in its place is a lesson you'll need to revisit again and again.

Rights and Responsibilities

In this lesson students create a bill of rights for using technology in the classroom; see the example in Figure 4.2. For younger students this list may be

Rights of Technology Users	Responsibilities of Technology Users
• We have the right to be creative with our tools. • We have the right to get help when we need it. • We have the right to positive conversations and feedback. • We have the right to be treated with courtesy in the digital classroom. • We have the right to critique tools and give suggestions for how to improve them or their use.	• We have the responsibility to care for our devices and follow rules. • We are responsible for doing our best work. • We are responsible for helping one another and sharing our ideas. • We are responsible for being innovative with our tools. • We are responsible for our words and work; we recognize that work published on the Internet is public.

Figure 4.2 Rights and Responsibilities of Technology Users

short; older students may have a lot to say. (We connect this list to the "Rights and Responsibilities of Readers" chart we've created with students during reading workshop.)

Why Teach This Lesson?

This lesson gets at the core of what is commonly called digital citizenship. It's important for even our youngest students to understand that stepping into a digital community comes with responsibility. At the same time, they also have rights they can expect others in the class to respect and guard.

Lead-In

If you've done a similar lesson with your readers, writers, or mathematicians, have the chart handy to refer to as an example. Students with a lot of experience in using technology will generate many elements, but others may need prompting; you may want to have a list already created to scaffold student thinking.

Teach

"What responsibilities do you have when you pick up a piece of technology? What about when you are interacting with classmates or friends on a device?

How might your responsibilities be different at school than at home? How are they the same?"

* * *

"What rights do you have as a digital citizen? Can people take your photo and post it without permission? What about your privacy? How can you expect to be treated when you're participating in an online community?"

Remember and Reteach

You'll come back to this lesson often during the year. Teachers have a responsibility to make sure students know how to be kind, productive, and upstanding users of technology. Intentionally or not, students will make mistakes and poor choices. Revisit and reteach until they get it. Digital citizenship is like any other classroom skill; when students don't grasp it, continue to reteach until they do. As students gain skills, the complexity of what they are able to do will deepen. We find ways to continually build on previous lessons throughout the year.

Troubleshooting 101

In this lesson you create a troubleshooting chart for students to follow when something isn't working properly. Elicit students' own experiences when something has gone wrong and create a flowchart of steps to take in these situations. You may be able to create a list quickly if your students have past experiences with technology; if not, look at the chart as a work in progress and add to it as things come up during the year.

Why Teach This Lesson?

You can't stop and fix a problem every time it arises. This lesson establishes a mindset of students helping students and prompts them to look for solutions to problems before asking you for help. When you put supports in place and teach kids to use one another as resources, you have more time for instruction. Every minute you don't spend demonstrating again how to save a piece of work is one you can use to confer, assess, and instruct small groups. The specifics of the lesson will depend on the types of devices you have, how many, and your district's technology guidelines.

Lead-In
You'll prepare two charts during this lesson. The first lists general trouble-shooting steps; see Figure 4.3. The second is a known issues and specialists chart, which you'll add to during the year.

Teach
"Today I want to share with you how we do something called troubleshooting. Troubleshooting is trying different approaches to solve a problem. It's similar to how we guess and check in math. As we learn about tools, we'll add more tips to our chart, but there are a few things we can talk about to get started. Has anyone had experience with doing this kind of troubleshooting before? Turn and talk about some technology problems you've had and how you solved them. Then we'll put together some suggestions we can follow when we're having technology issues."

* Quit the app or program completely and restart it.
* Log out and log back in.
* Reload the page.
* Look on with a buddy until a teacher can assist you.
* Turn off the device and turn it back on.
* Check your Wi-Fi connection.
* Ask a friend.
* Check the known issues chart and consult a specialist.
* Move near the cart so you can plug in.
* If you're in the middle of a lesson, grab a clipboard and paper so you can still jot your thinking.

Figure 4.3 Troubleshooting Tips

Remember and Reteach

As issues come up during the year, have students add to the known issues chart and list themselves as specialists. This encourages student independence and leaves you more time to teach.

Students as Specialists

You want to establish a way for students who have discovered tips and tricks to share them with the class. One way is on a specialists-in-the-classroom bulletin board. Another is a weekly slam in which students share a tip, trick, or a special skill orally. You don't have to limit the specialist board to technology—including skills in all areas lets every student identify an area of proficiency. Perhaps Sophia is skilled at helping readers find fantasy books, Bran is great at visual strategies for problem solving, Martine is a master of iMovie, and Angelo is savvy about video blogs.

Why Teach This Lesson?

Allowing students to step into the role of classroom specialists empowers them to own the learning and take on the role of teacher as well as student. This creates a classroom where every student is honored for their knowledge and skill set.

Lead-In

Decide how you will feature your classroom specialists. The easiest way is by creating a specialists bulletin board or chart; see Figure 4.4. You could post student photographs and have kids add small badges or index cards underneath their names stating the things they are expert in. Start with anything, whether it applies to what you do in class or not, then move on to classroom skills as the year progresses.

Teach

"What do you know a lot about? What do you feel you can teach your class-mates about? Write or draw that on the index card I gave you and post it under your picture on our specialists bulletin board."

* * *

Figure 4.4 A First-Grade "We Are Specialists" Chart at the Beginning of the Year

"I love that you discovered how to do that! Let's add that to your expert topics on the board.

Hey class, Jack just figured out how to fix the issue some of you have been having. Come on over to the carpet and he'll give you a quick lesson."

* * *

"I'm sure we have an expert in the class who knows how to fix that. Check the specialists board and see whether a classmate can help you out."

Remember and Reteach

If a student is overwhelmed by requests for her expertise, have her train a team of experts, perhaps one student from each table or desk group. Every kid in your class can be a specialist! This is often most important for students who don't fit easily into the social fabric of the class. Latching onto their successes, no matter how small, and holding them up as leaders in the classroom builds their self-esteem and sense of belonging within the community.

Safeguarding Our Intellectual Property

Even the youngest students can begin to explore the idea of intellectual property. Who owns the work is a hot topic in today's superconnected world. By introducing this concept, you'll help your learners see that their work is valued and deserves attribution, just as they must give credit to words and images they find in books and media.

Why Teach This Lesson?

Early lessons on ownership and fair use of work lay important groundwork. In an age in which copying and pasting are the norm and plagiarism is easier than ever, it's essential that students understand how and why to credit people for their work.

Lead-In

Have several pieces of student work—writing, artwork, or other original material—on hand to use as a jumping-off point to discuss ownership and attribution. Starting this discussion with student work makes the issue personal and helps students understand why attribution is so important.

Teach

"I think it would be great if we published our poems along with the photographs that inspired them. One thing that's really important is making sure we give credit to the person who took the photograph, so we're going to include a photo credit underneath."

* * *

"How does it make you feel to see that you've been given credit for your work? Why do you think it's important for us to give credit for images or words that we use from books or the Internet?"

* * *

"Turn and talk about this word, plagiarism. *Have you heard this word before? What does it mean? How would you feel if*

In this lesson we also talk with students about how they can keep themselves safe online. We explicitly teach them not to post photos of themselves on their blog. If they are sharing their work online, we teach them to color over a photo or use *image stamping* (see http://bit .ly/1JMM4AJ).

you went on the Internet and saw someone else was taking credit for something you made or wrote?"

Remember and Reteach

You'll teach this lesson again and again as students move through the year and begin to explore projects where they may want to use materials they find on the Internet. We remind them that we cannot use these items without permission, then direct them to sites providing images and music for fair use, have them work with the art teacher to develop needed skills, and introduce them to a variety of creative apps and tools to help them develop their own images, music, and content for their projects.

The Priority Hierarchy

This lesson establishes priorities to help students focus their technology use. For example, students could spend hours playing with fonts instead of writing. Present various scenarios and have students talk through which things are important to focus on and which they should save for another time.

Why Teach This Lesson?

When we asked students to type a quick digital response, we often saw them spend ten minutes picking out a font; typing some text and centering it for no apparent reason; making the text larger, then smaller, and then huge before making it smaller again; changing the color of the font five times; forgetting to type their name; and then rushing to finish because they spent so much time fiddling with the format. Everything students publish doesn't have to be in 12-point Times New Roman, but they need to understand that content is most important and that creative embellishments need to serve a purpose.

Lead-In

Since the hierarchy will change with what you are doing in class and the tools you are using, you need an anchor lesson that applies to any situation. A pyramid (see Figure 4.5) or timeline gives students a visual representation of how much time they should spend on each element, either by class period or over

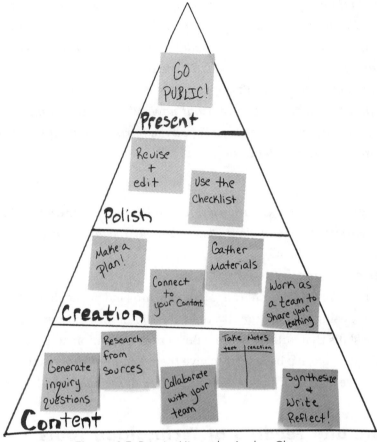

Figure 4.5 Priority Hierarchy Anchor Chart

days and weeks (for longer projects). Always include students in the discussion of what goes where and how much time they should spend on each element of an assignment so they begin to internalize these structures.

Teach

"I have to tell you a story. Last night I was trying to work on an important document, but I kept getting distracted. First the dog was barking so I took him out, then I spent a long time playing with the format, then I started working on the title page, then I went to do some dishes, and then I checked my email. It was a disaster. I barely got anything done. Does this ever happen to you?

"I think it might help to use a priority hierarchy. A hierarchy is something that groups things in order of importance. I needed to do that last night. All of those things I spent time on weren't really important. What I needed to do was sit down and start writing, but instead I spent my time on other parts of my project and my life that weren't important.

"Let's apply this to our classroom right now. What are we working on that could use a priority makeover? Let's list all the parts or steps of that project and then rank them in order of importance."

* * *

"This looks great! Let's make sure we refer back to this every day and use it to guide how we spend time in class. This will really recharge our work."

Remember and Reteach

You may have to revisit this chart again and again (and yet again with certain students). But being able to organize their time, minimize distractions, and be efficient are skills that will carry them far in their education and their life. If students really struggle, it's beneficial to give them a miniature version of the chart that they can keep in their notebook or tape to their desk as a ready reminder.

The Care and Feeding of Technology Tools

This lesson establishes norms for handling, using, caring for, and storing devices. (In the early elementary grades, you may need to present this over a period of several days.) It sets the foundation for the rest of the year, so be explicit and have students practice the behavior. Specify how students should carry devices, where they should store devices when not in use, when they may use them, expectations for cleaning screens and headphones, and any other day-to-day operations you need to establish.

Why Teach This Lesson?

This lesson is essential. Your students need a shared understanding about device management so you can focus on more important things. It also helps preserve expensive equipment.

Figure 4.6 A Student Tech Team Member Charges Devices at the End of the Day

Lead-In

Before you teach this lesson, collaborate with your colleagues on school-wide expectations. School-wide norms deepen students' understanding of why these expectations and practices are necessary. They also promote effective modeling and monitoring. You might take photos of people (teachers and students) demonstrating proper handling techniques (a two-hand hold, for example) to add to your classroom chart.

Teach

"This morning I caught my husband working on his computer with a cup of coffee in his hand. It reminded me of how careful we have to be. We have to take care of our technology devices so they remain useful all year long and in future years. Can you remember any of our school's guidelines for using technology?"

* * *

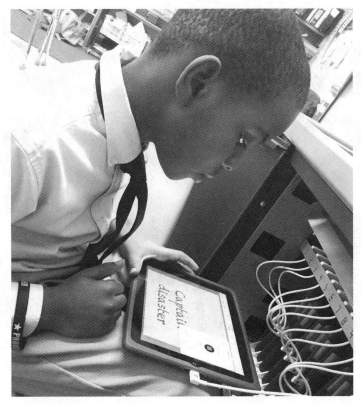

Figure 4.7 A Student Powers Up His iPad

"That's great! We need to think about these things as well:

- *How should we carry it?*
- *When should we clean our devices?*
- *When is it OK to do maintenance like deleting photos or changing the background?*
- *How shall we store them when not in use?*
- *What do we need to remember to do every night before we leave?"*

Remember and Reteach

Include any accessories such as stands and headphones in this lesson. Take photos of students demonstrating proper use and handling to hang with your anchor chart as visual reminders. Students love to see themselves represented

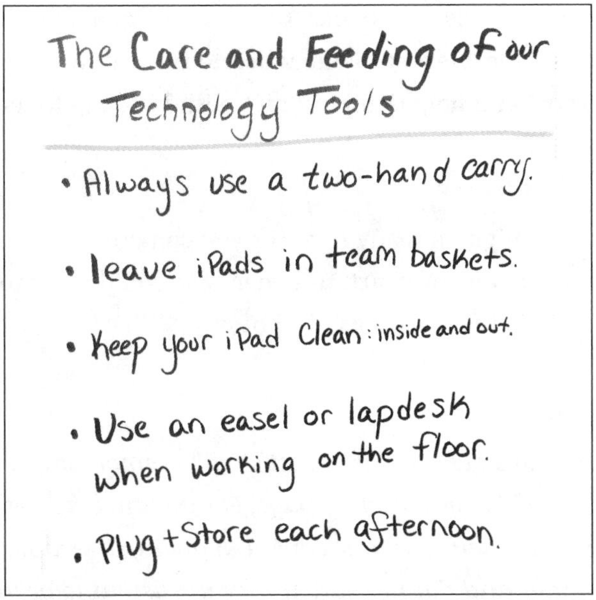

Figure 4.8 "The Care and Feeding of Our Technology Tools" Chart

in teaching tools, and the visual reminders stand out from a sea of words on anchor charts.

Classroom Signals

Create common signals to aid device management and workflow:

- a hand signal and phrase for when you need students' complete attention (We say, "Screens down," and turn one hand palm down.)
- a signal students use to indicate their technology is not working (This differentiates tech questions from content questions, so you can send a classroom helper.)
- a ready signal (We use a thumbs-up.)

Why Teach This Lesson?

Teaching kids to use and respond to hand signals minimizes distractions so you can maximize instruction. Kids need to move around quickly and effectively, carrying devices, clipboards, and books. Classroom signals distinguish instructional from creative time, alert students when to interact with their peers and when to listen to you, and help them interact with learning tools productively.

Lead-In

You may have a set of signals ready to go, or you can create them with students and record them on an anchor chart. In either case you'll want to display them on a chart with reinforcing drawings or photos.

Teach

"Friends, when we have our devices out, it's really important to use some signals that help us all be on the same page. For instance, sometimes I notice people already getting their iPad out when I'm giving directions, or I see people typing on a computer and I'm not sure if they are listening or not. So we need a quick way to signal that it's time to stop, look, and listen. What signal should we use for this? What else might we use?"

* * *

"Great! Let me jot those down on our chart so we can remember them."

* * *

"Where should our devices be, or how should we hold them, to signal we are ready to listen?"

* * *

"What other technology signals might we need? How about when you can't get something to work and you need help?"

Remember and Reteach

Model and reteach this concept often until students internalize it. Have them also use these signals when they are working in groups. There are many times throughout the day when it's important to set technology aside, look one another in the eye, and have face-to-face conversations.

Surfing the Net

Collaborate on a classroom chart that students can refer to as they search for online content at school. Discuss what to do if students access a blocked site or stumble on inappropriate content.

Why Teach This Lesson?

The purpose of this lesson is twofold: you'll introduce students to school and district policies regarding technology and establish baseline expectations for using technology in class. When you co-construct guidelines with your students, they understand the expectations and own the norms set by the group. Students will be challenged by the Internet at some point. Teach them to anticipate a few of these challenges ahead of time so they'll know what to do.

Lead-In

Prepare a version of your school's or district's policy on Internet use in student-friendly language. Create an anchor chart highlighting some of the most important points, but leave room for students to add their own guidelines for your classroom.

Teach

"These are some of the very important guidelines that we need to follow in order to use technology in our classroom. What do you notice about them? Which ones do you have questions about?"

* * *

"I'm wondering if we can think of some of our own guidelines that are special for our classroom. What do you think? Turn and talk to your partner and then let's share as a class."

* * *

"Great; let's hear your ideas. You talk and I'll jot them down in my notebook. Then we can reread them and decide which ones we want to add to our chart."

District policy is often too complex for primary-grade students. Instead, you could assemble a list of accessible, safe places for them to find information online (see Figure 4.9).

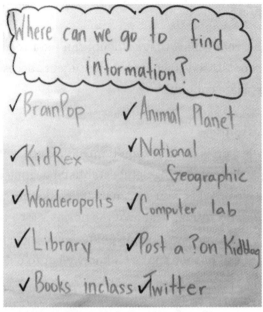

Figure 4.9 "Where Can We Go to Find Information?" Chart

Remember and Reteach

You will edit, add to, or change this chart during the year. Refer students to it when they forget and talk about why the guidelines are in place.

Naming and Sharing Work

There are many ways to manage getting files and work to and from students—Dropbox folders, learning management systems, syncing, Google Drive accounts, email, and the list goes on. How you share depends on the work you are doing, how large the files are, the equipment and programs your school provides, whom you are sharing with, and what is easiest to manage.

Start the year with a lesson on how students are to email work to you and how you want them to name files. This differs by grade and often depends on whether your students have school-issued email accounts or not. If students do not have email accounts, use platforms that do not require login. Teach the youngest learners how to use the email feature in one lesson, and in a later lesson teach them how to add their name or device number to the subject line.

Have students with a school-issued email address put their device number, name, and a short description of what they are sending in the subject line. Using the same convention to name files keeps it simple. File names should include the following:

In our school K–2 students don't use email addresses; instead, all devices in the primary grades have a school-issued email address. The devices can send a file or image from within an app or as a photo, but students don't email back and forth with their teachers or peers.

- device number or name (We often assign students a numbered device, which they use all the time.)
- student name
- classroom number or period (if using shared devices)
- subject or assignment

Prepare a chart listing the various ways students can share work with you—email, link or upload to a learning management system, post on their blog, and so on. Add to it during the year as they learn new tools.

List your naming and sharing requirements on a large chart (see Figure 4.10) in a readily visible place; students will need time for this to become automatic.

Why Teach This Lesson?

It's essential that we develop easy to manage systems for students to share their work with us and each other. Gathering student work can become

---

How to Name and Share Your Files

* In order, type: device number, first name, assignment (for example: 6JulieMathReflection).

* Then check the board for instructions on how you should share today.

Figure 4.10 Naming and Sharing Work

time-consuming and overwhelming if we let it. Setting up these procedures will ensure that work flow is simple and organized.

Lead-In

Have your anchor chart with how to name files ready to go, along with a simple assignment (a brief description of the book they are currently reading, for example, or anything relevant to that day's classwork) for students to complete and send to you. This lets them practice naming the document and sending an email. If students have assigned devices, keep a list handy for reference. If not, ask them to use the number of whatever device they are working on, so you can track the work if you need to.

Teach

"When you send me work, it's important that you name your files in a special way so that I can keep everything organized. I've shown you on this chart how I'd like for you to do it."

* * *

"OK. You've typed a few sentences about what you're reading right now. Go ahead and save your document the way I showed you."

* * *

Because saving methods depend on the device, program, or app being used, this part will vary. You might take photographs of those your students commonly use and add them to the chart. You might also document where to change the file name on apps, since they frequently automatically save work.

"Great. Now I want you to send it to me via email. You'll see I've written my email address on the board. Make sure to write a subject line using the same format so I know what you're sending me and whom it's from."

Remember and Reteach

Hang your chart where it's easily visible to students. Small laminated copies of all your anchor charts are very helpful for those learners who may need a personal copy. Or print stickers and place them on the back of index cards or in notebooks for kids to quickly reference. (Kids can punch holes in cards and keep them on a ring for easy reference.)

What Looks the Same?

This lesson makes students aware of symbols common to many technology platforms. Create an anchor chart with students that helps them recognize, name, and use these symbols as they interact with new apps and websites during the year. Update the chart as students learn new tools.

Why Teach This Lesson?

Knowing these symbols helps students explore a new application. When students know that a plus sign typically means to start something new or that a square with an upward arrow emerging from it means to send or share, they become more autonomous when using new programs and platforms. They have a tool kit for getting started and can move forward with increased independence.

Lead-In

Display a piece of chart paper titled "Technology Symbols We Know." Have your iPad next to you to refer to as you demonstrate, using an app or a website students are already familiar with. Starting with technology students have used lets them be more involved in identifying and naming the symbols they know.

Teach

"When we explore a new app or investigate a website, there's often a lot to learn before we can use the tool effectively. To begin navigating a new tool, it's helpful if we can locate some symbols that we've seen and used in other applications or websites. For instance, when you see a triangle button pointing to the right, what does that mean? Play, right? If you wanted to pause that same video, what would you push? You'd tap the two little lines that are right next to each other, the pause button. Turn and talk with your partner about other apps or websites you've seen these buttons in."

* * *

"As we learn new apps and websites, use the tools and symbols you know in order to get started. Think about how you can learn more about the app by starting small and thinking about what makes sense."

Remember and Reteach

Hang the anchor chart (see Figure 4.11) where it is easily visible. This is a fluid support tool and should change and grow as the class learns more symbols during the year. Before sending students off to work independently, direct their attention to the chart and remind them to use what they know in order to get started.

Figure 4.11 Common Symbols for Apps

 Scan this QR code or visit http://hein.pub/amplify to see videos of teachers and students in action and access up-to-date resources for this book (use keycode AMPLIFY15).

Reflection and Assessment

Students bounce out of the classroom when the final bell rings, but our day is not over. From early in the morning until late into the evening, we find there are never enough hours or cups of coffee in our day. Still, it's important for us to sit and be calm for a few moments, to reflect on the day: choices we made, effectiveness of lessons, ideas for tomorrow. Of course reflection is a constant part of our day as we notice and note student responses and interactions. We reflect on how well prepared students are for a group discussion, how learners responded to a math lesson, or which strategies they applied in writing that day. Self-awareness and learning are driven by the power to identify what factors, tools, and learning activities are most engaging and most effective.

Several years into her technology journey, Katie began experimenting with Edmodo, excited by the idea of having a place for students to chat and collaborate online. However, she wanted to make sure the online collaboration added something she wouldn't have otherwise been able to do. She also wondered what additional information about students she might obtain. Looking at how students collaborated without technology, she noted that they worked in small groups, filled out graphic organizers, and turned and talked with classmates. Her goal was to build on and enhance those practices, not replace them.

The first few attempts were rough. Students were trying to figure out how to use the website, post their thinking, and have an online discussion all at one time. Katie and her students worked through these challenges and tweaked the process until they established a format and guidelines that worked for everyone.

The classroom dynamic changed; some students participated more in the digital format, while others took a step back. Elyza, who was often unsure of what to say, found that seeing examples of her classmates' work jump-started her thinking. After a few discussions, she moved from repeating comments to building on them with her own thinking. Franco preferred digital discussions because he never had enough time to say everything he wanted to in a turn-and-talk. But Natalie was frustrated; she took a long time to compose her responses, and the conversation had often moved on by the time she posted her thinking. Keisha craved the quick back-and-forth of a face-to-face conversation and the social connection she felt with other students in a small group.

Katie learned valuable lessons about how to best launch a new technological platform with her students and how she needed to prepare in order to make the lessons go smoothly. Through conversations, observations, and surveys (see Figure 5.1), she determined the balance her students needed between digital and traditional tools, what lessons she needed to teach explicitly, and what supports students required to be successful.

Digital Discussion Survey

* Required

Name *

[   ]

How did you feel your digital discussion went today?
Check all of the boxes that you feel describe your discussion

- ☐ exciting
- ☐ fast-paced
- ☐ thought-provoking
- ☐ slow
- ☐ supportive
- ☐ easy-going
- ☐ off topic
- ☐ not supportive
- ☐ engaging
- ☐ silly
- ☐ Other: [   ]

Talk about the things that went well in your discussion today. *

[   ]

What would make your discussion better next time? *

[   ]

Figure 5.1 An Online Student Survey   *(continues)*

Are there any areas either with technology or discussion that you have a question about? *

```



```

What is your goal for your next discussion? *

```



```

Submit

Figure 5.1 *continued*

Katie prefers digital reflections because it is easy for the students and her to compare responses over time. You can also use paper and pencil or any other method that's easy to manage.

The simple act of giving ourselves permission to stop and watch opens our eyes to the rich fabric of learning in our classroom. We can examine the quality of the tasks we ask our students to undertake. What impact do they have? Why is this important? How can this be better? Too often we get caught up in a Pinterest frenzy of creating bulletin boards or downloading worksheets with cute fonts. These things have little or no impact on student learning. What does is reflecting on our instruction, analyzing what works, discussing different approaches with our colleagues, evaluating student work, engaging students in reflection, and ultimately adjusting our practice.

Reflection—thinking through our choices before a lesson, observing students and looking at their work, analyzing the successful and not-so-successful elements of our instruction—drives good teaching, so we do a lot of it. Perhaps we have a fleeting thought while watching students navigate a tool for the first time: "Aha! I see what I should have done to make this clearer" or "My students are struggling; how can I push their thinking?" Or maybe we undertake a prolonged contemplation of student work: "When they blog about their reading, they write more and write more creatively. They report feeling motivated and excited about their work because they are connecting with an audience."

When we began using technology in our classrooms, we noticed the following:

- *We used technology to curate student learning.* We realized that we could use the power of technology to gather information about our students in new and multifaceted ways, in all areas of the curriculum, with both digital and traditional student work. Our data collection became more authentic, current, differentiated, rich, and efficient.

- *Technology changed our learning landscape.* Technology is a tool, not a panacea for fixing problems. When we first considered bringing technological tools into our classrooms, we saw a lot of examples of technology being used poorly. Why would we switch from an effective and proven instructional method that didn't use technology to a less effective one that did? We anchored it to what we knew about best-practice teaching and how it might enhance what we were already doing, so we could make informed decisions about when, why, where, and how best to use technology.

- *We expanded students' reflections on their learning to include their technology preferences and use.* Integral to this work was involving students in the reflection process. Their feedback on how things worked, what they learned, what they enjoyed, and what they struggled with as well as their ideas for the future were essential in crafting a rich learning experience. We pushed them

Reflection can take many forms. Ideally, you'll have time to reflect on your classroom work and that of your students with a team of colleagues. However, if you are unable to connect with others in your school, reach out to fellow teacher-learners online and find your tribe. There are thousands of teachers out there who would love to connect with you about the thinking and learning taking place in your classroom!

to identify their own strengths and needs in using technology as a tool for learning. We helped them make good choices. We listened to and involved them as we incorporated new tools into creative projects, daily classroom management, and workflow.

USE TECHNOLOGY TO CURATE STUDENT LEARNING

We learn so much by watching our students—how they approach a task and interact with materials, the pace at which they work, and so on. Do they take a few moments to gather their thoughts before starting? Do they look to their peers for support or prefer to work alone? Do they dive into a task headfirst with motivation and excitement or just want to be done? Students demonstrate their learning preferences in all areas of the curriculum and in their interactions with digital tools. We can use technology to find out more about our students than we've ever known before.

The ways in which teachers archive observations and thoughts are limitless. Some keep a notebook with a tab for each student or color-coded sheets on a clipboard. Note taking and data collection can be both a blessing and a curse, helpful and overwhelming. We've tried all manner of methods over the years, some more successfully than others. But as our classrooms have become more digital, so have our methods for archiving student work and our observations. We've harnessed the power of technology to become more efficient curators and reflectors.

Capturing Students as They Work

We don't sit at the front of our classrooms all day. Our classroom communities bustle with purpose and work, and we roam within them, observing, questioning, coaching, prompting, and sharing in the learning. As students collaborate, talk, write, solve problems, research, and experiment, we observe, jot these observations down, and use them to assess their current learning, how far they've progressed, and how we can personalize their learning to get them where they need to go. Taking pictures in the classroom has become a powerful tool, a new way to take notes. Over time, these snapshots give us information on the following:

- *Learning preferences*: Where do students sit? Whom do they work with? What tools are they consistently using?
- *Understanding*: Are students able to work with manipulatives? Sort fiction and nonfiction books? Write down their thinking? Document and reflect on day-to-day learning?
- *Student work*: A sentence worked especially hard on during writing workshop or a eureka moment during math highlights what students know and are able to do in a given moment.

Adding audio documentation makes these photos even more valuable. A brief recording capturing a conversation with a student, a comment, or an observation enhances this strategy. For example, we often snap pictures of students holding their current book and record a short bit of our conversation to document their thinking.

Benefiting from Students' Digital Work Products

When students use digital tools to capture and share their learning, they are doing much of the archival work for us. Think of the full understanding we have after we've reviewed our conference notes and snapshots, looked over a student's notebook, reviewed his contribution to a small-group digital conversation, watched his videotaped reflection, and assessed his digitally created nonfiction book.

Digital tools are also powerful vehicles for helping students reflect on their growth. A student-authored blog acts as a weekly archive of learning, and with the proper coaching, students can use their blog entries to identify patterns and set instructional goals. Students can review their previous video made in the recording studio while filling out a checklist (see Figure 5.2) to improve the content and technical skill of the next one.

At this point you might be asking yourself: "But doesn't this take a lot of time?" The answer is yes and no. As we use more technology in our classrooms

> * I can hear all my words; I spoke loudly and clearly.
>
> * I can see my whole face framed in the video; there are no distractions in the background.
>
> * I showed the book cover and gave important details, such as the title, the author, and the book bin it's in.
>
> * I told what happens in the book step-by-step.
>
> * I shared at least three pieces of my own thinking about the book, as well as the pages in the book that prompted those thoughts.

Figure 5.2 Reflection Checklist for a Book Review Video

we have to balance the time spent in teaching, managing, and assessing work product with the positive outcomes for students. The goal is not to add more work but to shift the work in a way that makes sense for you and your students.

Digital student work offers

- more and more varied work product from which to build an understanding of student learning.
- enhanced curating and organization possibilities as student work is collected through blogs, shared folders, and other digital portfolio systems.
- share-ability among students, teachers, and families.

We've found that involving students in self-assessment and reflection, peer conferences, and work storage is a fantastic way to keep them at the center of their own learning as well as help us manage digital artifacts effectively. In short, we don't do anything that we can teach students to do for themselves.

We don't view every single student video on a daily basis, but instead use a work sampling approach where we view a variety of pieces to gather feedback and help plan future instruction. However, when we do need to look at additional evidence of learning it's all right there.

For more detailed strategies, thoughts, and ideas you can read our blog series on "Making Digital Artifacts Work" at http://bit.ly/1f5fBKA .

CHANGE THE LEARNING LANDSCAPE

How do the choices and experiences we give our students help them learn? When we use technology in our classrooms, we must examine carefully how that use impacts our students' learning. As our Twitter friend Tony Keefer once said, "Is the juice worth the squeeze?" Is what we put into technology worth what we and our students get out of it? We might observe the class with the following questions in mind:

- *How comfortable are students with using technology?* Students come to us with a wide range of background experiences and abilities. Some use technology as easily and intuitively as they do paper and pencil. Others may struggle with general familiarity or the size of the device or skills such as keyboarding or navigating a touch screen. Still others may have special needs that impair their ability to use or participate in technologically driven learning experiences. Whatever the need, our job is to ensure that all students have access and the ability to participate. We therefore provide instruction and alternative choices or tools when needed. We also involve and collaborate with special educators, technology teachers, and school media specialists.

- *How quickly do students become proficient with new tools?* We know it often feels like students get it faster than we do some days. But that isn't necessarily the case. We need to pay careful attention to how quickly students pick up techniques and tools, discover tool functions, and brainstorm new ways to use them. Some students use technology naturally; these specialists help us raise the level of work in our classroom. The amount of time it takes to launch a new tool determines whether it's worth doing so. Teaching is a delicate balance of skills and strategies, instruction and assessment, and there is never enough time. So if we're going to spend time getting our students to use a tool proficiently, the payoff needs to be big.

- *To what degree do students participate in online interactions?* Although some students who excel at face-to-face interaction also excel at digital communication, some do not. Students who have a great deal to say orally may need more time to compose their thinking in a digital format and feel left behind when the rest of the group is already well into the conversation. Small groups work best for these conversations; sometimes grouping students by their interaction rate puts them at ease and they feel more confident.

- *Can they transfer skills from nontechnological to technological contexts?* Knowledge transfer is the ultimate evidence that students have internalized and can apply new learning. We teach students to annotate articles or jot thinking on sticky notes when they read nonfiction. We encourage them to use reading strategies to monitor comprehension, ask questions, and synthesize information. When the medium switches to images, video, or online text, how well are they able to transfer these skills? Do they use effective research strategies in the library but struggle on the Internet? Do they communicate and collaborate effectively face-to-face but get lost during digital interactions? We need to help them make these connections through explicit instruction and modeling.

- *Does their proficiency change when using technology?* Some students suddenly stop using punctuation when they move from handwriting to typing. When students begin using technology, they may appear to abandon skills they once had or demonstrate skills not previously evident. Students use writing, talking, recording, and drawing to communicate. If their proficiency decreases when the tool changes, we must observe carefully how that tool may be affecting them. If they struggle no matter the format, intervention may be necessary.

EXPAND STUDENT SELF-REFLECTION

No discussion of reflection is complete without talking about the role students play. Self-reflection is an important step in taking ownership of one's learning. Research reveals that students who reflect on practices and strategies perform better in both the short and long terms (Fondas 2014). We ask students to reflect on their choices, skills, strategies, and growth in all areas of the curriculum. We should embed self-reflection in our technology curriculum as well. We want students to consider how technology might help or hinder their process, which platforms and apps work best for them, and what areas they need to work on.

Technology also helps our students gather data about themselves as learners. Whether they are photos of their work, a detailed portfolio, or a digital record of daily progress, these footprints of learning are rich in information students can use to evaluate their own progress (Pahomov 2014).

To know how well we are mastering something, we need to understand what we are working toward. During a small-group discussion, there are qualities each student strives for—be prepared by doing all the reading, make eye contact with the speaker, talk about the text and give examples of what you mean, disagree agreeably. At the end, students reflect on how well they did. Identifying what makes a successful discusser, reader, writer, or problem solver and then helping students work toward those ideals is a safe and supportive way for kids to own what they need to do to be stronger learners. We can and should apply this same strategy to technology.

To create shared expectations for using technology, we need to

- include students' observations, thoughts, and ideas;
- present examples for students to examine;
- make expectations for learning visible and accessible through tools like anchor charts;
- provide ample opportunities for students to revisit and reflect on expectations; and
- adjust expectations as the year continues in order to help students grow.

This takes us beyond the initial lessons on proper use into the nuances of specific tools, apps, or projects—transferring small-group discussion skills to an online discussion or establishing guidelines for sharing mathematical thinking through screencasts (a digital recording that captures action taking place on a student device), for example.

Daily Reflection

Kids need to reflect early and often in order to take small steps forward in learning. Establishing a system for daily reflection prompts them to set small, attainable goals and gather their thoughts about their progress over time, so by the time they receive our assessment, they already have a strong idea of what they've learned and what they'd like to learn next. We want kids to know what they know and what they don't know; what they are good at and which skills to target the next time around; where they are and where they need to be. Following are some ways we can help students reflect using both digital and nondigital tools. As you consider these options, evaluate whether students will be able to review their reflections, whether they will be public or private, and whether they can become part of a long-term reflection portfolio.

Sticky Notes in a Folder

This system is appropriate for learners of all ages. A file folder houses sticky notes on which students jot down various skills and strategies they are working on, one per sticky note. (Our littlest learners sometimes draw images.) We may suggest a skill to add based on our observations. Sometimes we use just the two sides of the folder (see Figure 5.3); other times we designate three or four sections (see Figure 5.4). The students move their sticky notes across the columns as they demonstrate mastery. The format is flexible and easy to individualize, and the physical act of moving a sticky note from the "Working on It" to the "Got It" section is sometimes just the feedback a kid needs. We keep folders in an easy-to-reach place.

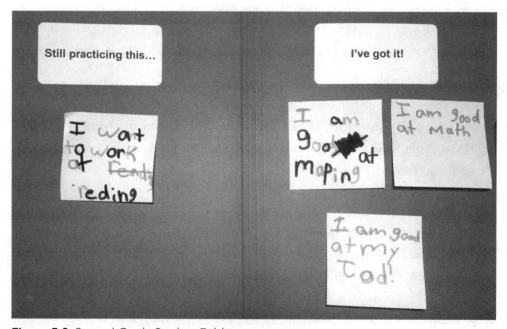

Figure 5.3 Second-Grade Student Folder

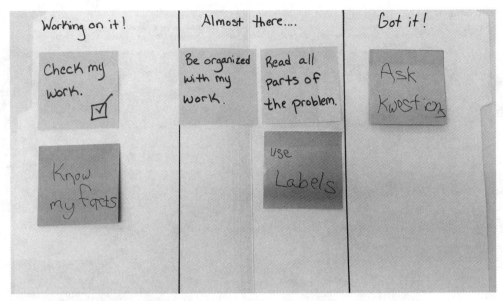

Figure 5.4 Fifth-Grade Student Folder

Digital Stickies

Using the same basic principle of the folder, students can maintain a digital "wall" or "corkboard" of stickies or cards (see Figure 5.5). Individual students can have their own, with customized backgrounds to mimic a folder, or a group of students can share one, to collect reflections (see Figure 5.6). This digital version allows students to color-code and move things around easily, and it's more durable than a folder (students can refer back to digital stickies over months or years). It's also easy to share with group members, teachers, and parents. Depending on the program or app (we've used Padlet, Corkulous, Popplet, and a number of others), it may also be possible to embed links, images, or videos. Choose one that's easy to access and easy for students to use. For some other tool suggestions, see http://bit.ly/1FVodcf.

Section in a Notebook

Students insert a tab in the back of their notebook and enter short reflections there. They write the date in the margin and may use a variety of sentence stems to get started (see Figure 5.7). Sometimes students select a stem appropriate for the day's learning; other times we ask the entire class to use the same

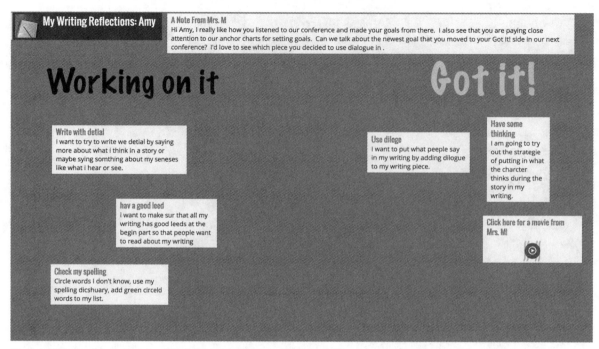

Figure 5.5 Padlet Reflection Wall: Individual (To view this wall online, visit http://bit.ly/1IK1uqw.)

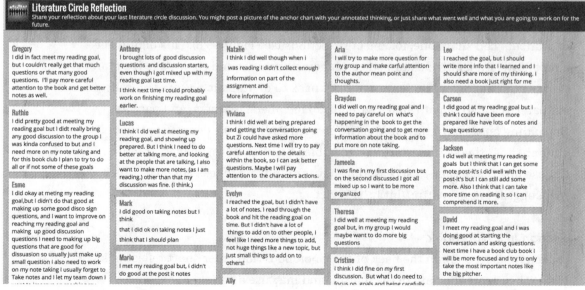

Figure 5.6 Padlet Reflection Wall: Group (To view this wall online, visit http://bit.ly/1Fbn0gf.)

> * Today I was proud of _____.
>
> * The most challenging thing for me today was _____. The strategies I used to overcome it were _____.
>
> * I have a question about _____.
>
> * The steps I took to reach my goal today were _____.
>
> * I was successful in _____. I still need to work on _____.
>
> * Next time I think I should try _____.
>
> * I need help with _____.

Figure 5.7 Sentence Stems for Notebook Reflections

stem so everyone focuses on a particular area. Students may share what they've written with the class or with a partner.

Photos of Work Annotated with a Student's Thinking

Teachers cannot be in two (or thirty-two!) places at once. Classroom activities such as using math manipulatives to represent one's thinking or documenting how one sorted animals based on their habitats are ripe for photo annotation. To assess whether her students can identify the characteristics of fiction and nonfiction, Kristin has them snap quick photos of the covers of books in the classroom library. They open the photos in a drawing app and label each book with the category it falls into. They snap pictures of stacks of Unifix cubes and label them to show which are odd and which are even. They also create visual book reviews by snapping a selfie of their favorite "right now" title and labeling it with words, doodles, and stickers to show how they'd rate it.

Older students might capture a model of a fraction problem, add it to a digital book of images, and enter reflections about what they found challenging, what they learned, and what they still don't quite understand. Or they might take a screenshot of a website they found useful in their research on the American Revolution and annotate it with a short explanation of how well they think the site fits into the class guidelines for just-right websites. Perhaps they photograph a class checklist and use a drawing app to add a quick check-in (see Figure 5.8). They can email or upload these photos to a shared folder or store them in a photo roll (photo album on a student device); the quick addition of a date helps them track progress over time.

Exit Tickets on Index Cards

A simple way to gather feedback at the end of a lesson is to have students share their learning by writing a few sentences on an index card or a sticky note. (Younger learners may draw or write.) We're looking for evidence of thinking, not evaluating spelling or writing ability. Many times these exit slips guide our teaching throughout the year. Simple questions like "What did you learn? What do you wonder?" elicit feedback that helps us plan tomorrow's lesson with the

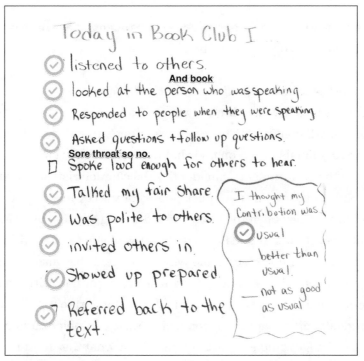

Figure 5.8 Annotated Anchor Chart (Taken from *Teaching for Comprehending and Fluency* by Irene C. Fountas and Gay Su Pinnell. Copyright © 2006 by Irene C. Fountas and Gay Su Pinnell. Published by Heinemann, Portsmouth, NH. All rights reserved.)

added benefit that we are carving out time for students to stop and reflect on their own learning. You can file cards or pass them back to students with a few short comments so kids can archive them in a way that makes sense for them.

Digital Exit Tickets

You can use a simple discussion tool like TodaysMeet as a digital exit slip even when there is only one device in the classroom. Students post their reflection to a discussion stream personalized for your class and available on any platform. TodaysMeet captures 140 characters of text and can be quickly switched from user to user by refreshing the URL. Kids rotate through this station, reflecting on their learning and moving on to the next task. Some of our colleagues use this tool to keep a running status of the class regarding independent reading; students can access and reflect on it at any time during the week.

We often have students take a photo of what they've worked on and then use the ChatterPix app to audio record up to thirty seconds of reflection on their learning. This app allows the viewer to see the image and hear the recording at the same time, thus giving us layered insight into student thinking. Tellagami is a similar tool for the thirty-second exit slip: students create an avatar, add an image, and record an audio comment about what they learned or noticed about themselves as a learner during the day's lesson.

Digital exit tickets don't have to be complex. When devices are limited, we snap photos of students as they give a thumb check or make a face showing how they felt while doing the lesson (see Figure 5.9). We can review the images later in the day as one more piece of evidence to assess student learning. Often we combine these images into a quick slideshow that we use to launch the next day's lesson, reminding students of the learning from the previous day and helping them reenter the experience right where they left off.

To gather feedback when there are lots of devices in the classroom, we use Google Forms, like the one in Figure 5.1. Students can submit their feedback online using any device, and the platform displays the responses on an easy-to-view spreadsheet. We're able to select various styles of student response: multiple choice, choose from a list, a free-form paragraph. Open-ended responses give a better snapshot of how our students approached the lesson and what they know and are able to do.

Figure 5.9 Students Offer Thumb Checks and Facial Responses

Long-Term Reflection

Students can easily turn these daily reflections into a more detailed reflection. For example, they might

- look at a series of sticky notes or other short notes and reflect on their growth over time;
- create a movie of snapshots of their work over time and record a voiceover highlighting what they learned;
- use their folder or virtual corkboard as a jumping-off point for a longer written or video reflection piece on long-term growth; or
- build a dynamic portfolio using keynote slides (see below).

Each fall Kristin shows her students how to use Apple's Keynote app to create slides containing photos and text. She models writing about a photo and invites students to choose images they've taken that represent their learning and thinking regarding various subjects. Students create keynotes (see the example in Figure 5.10) every other week as a way to reflect on their past

Sonic boom

March 21, 2012 @ 9:55 AM   _2 Comments_   _Edit this Post_

A sonic boom is if something goes faster then the sped of sound.
And when a sonic boom happens it makes a cloud and it's very loud.
The sped of is 700 miles an hour.
In the air show the planes can't do a sonic boom, it coud sacke windows.

---

2 Comments

This is my sonic boom blog.
It's my longest blog.

Figure 5.10 Adam's Sonic Boom Keynote

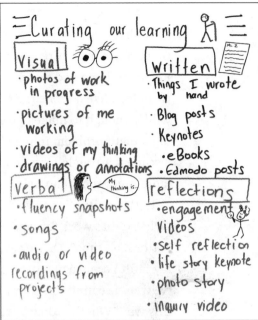

Figure 5.11 "Curating Our Learning" Chart

learning and summarize what they know across the curriculum. In a follow-up minilesson, Kristin teaches the term *curate* (see Figure 5.11) and prompts her students to archive meaningful work samples, ideas, and reflections for the long term. When someone discovers a new feature of the Keynote app, Kristin calls the class together and has this student share what she or he has learned. This authentic student-led minilesson builds student agency and identifies specialists or "student-teachers" who can support learning when Kristin is conferring with other students.

Over time, each self-curated keynote portfolio captures an authentic history of that child as a thinker, learner, and member of the first-grade classroom community. Kristin has her students look back and ask: "What do I notice about my thinking now compared with how I used to think? How has my work changed over the school year? What do I plan to learn next?" Students export their portfolios to the iBooks shelf (digital library on an iPad) as PDFs, and at the end of the school year, Kristin converts them into formats parents can access.

Process Reflections

Sometimes things don't work out the way we envisioned. It might be something that affects the entire class, a small group, or individuals. It's a horrible feeling to sit down and watch thirty video book reviews, only to find that most of them look like a scene from *The Blair Witch Project*, the camera having tilted wildly enough to make one seasick. Or observe a screencast of a student solving a math problem in which he hasn't narrated any of his thinking. Or watch a student struggle repeatedly with a particular app or platform, the technology more hindrance than help.

In these situations, we don't stop with "It didn't work." We ask students, "What didn't work for you? How can we fix this? What can we do to make it better next time?" Or we say, "Friends, yesterday didn't go well. I'm sorry; it's my fault because my instructions weren't as clear as they needed to be when we were learning this new app. Let's have another go, but this time let's try it this way." Whether they are five or fifteen, our students guide how we present a minilesson and the tools we use to capture thinking; they tell us what they need as learners to be more successful in the future. Struggle is learning. Failure is an opportunity to teach kids thoughtful persistence, a problem-solving mindset, and emotional fortitude.

Turning Reflections into Reviews

Any Internet search will produce a multitude of sites where people are spouting their opinions on everything under the sun—some useful, some spiteful, and others downright humorous. However, there is value in the idea of crowdsourcing—gathering the opinions, knowledge, and experience of many. When traveling, we often consult the website Yelp to find good restaurants. Detailed reviews that include dishes on the menu, ambience, and quality of service are the most helpful. In the same way, inviting students to review the technological tools they are using—what makes them valuable, easy to work with, useful, fun—is incredibly illuminating. These reviews create a shared vision of what learning looks like. They can be in writing (digital or by hand) or in a multimedia presentation. Writing app reviews is an authentic way for students to practice informational or argumentative writing. In a "battle of the apps," students debate the merit of apps designed to do similar jobs, comparing them point by point from functionality to cost. Going public with these reviews gives students the added benefit of knowing that their work is helping others.

Model and Support

Discuss what reviews should include, read or view mentor reviews, and model writing one. Then have students practice in pairs, giving feedback to each other and reflecting on what went well and how they can improve their next review. Display anchor charts and examples that students can revisit again and again as they work. Give students who need extra help a checklist to use as they compose their reviews.

Push Metacognition

As students work, you will want to listen in, read over their shoulders, and confer. The purpose is to evaluate the tool against specific criteria and craft a review with a specific purpose and audience in mind. Push even your youngest learners to say more than "I like this app because it's fun."

Go Public

Connecting with an audience is essential. Reviews are meant to be read. Make them as public as you can: share them with your personal learning network, other classrooms and schools, and app developers, and encourage thoughtful, kind feedback from these recipients.

Three Things to Try Tomorrow

Student Reflection Form

Use a digital tool like SurveyMonkey or Google Forms to gather feedback from students in addition to your classroom observations and conversations—how they feel about their progress or challenges, their peer collaborations, their interests for a topic of study, or a goal they've accomplished. Having members of a small group (book club, inquiry circle, etc.) use a form helps you monitor whether all students are contributing and all ideas are being heard, as well as identify misconceptions or misunderstandings. Or use a survey to gather information and reflections about technology tools. Ask students what questions they have, if there are areas of struggle, and what their ideas are for future uses.

Mini App Review

Introduce the idea of student-written reviews using a mini app review (or website or tool). Inspired by eight-word memoirs and three-word book reviews, we like to do a five-word app review. Students select five words to sum up an app and then write, draw, or paste the words on an image. You can have students take a photo of themselves with the tool, use a screenshot, or use the app icon. A vocabulary chart like the one in Figure 5.12 helps students expand their word choice and encourages metacognition.

Audio Snapshot

Have students use a free audio-recording tool like Vocaroo to record a thirty-second exit slip stating what they learned or wondered during a lesson. As a next step, invite students to use the recording tool to plan one or two things they want to do next time. When they listen to their recording the following day, they'll be reminded of their goals and can immediately focus on next steps.

Figure 5.12 Vocabulary Chart for Five-Word App Reviews

 Scan this QR code or visit http://hein.pub/amplify to see videos of teachers and students in action and access up-to-date resources for this book (use keycode AMPLIFY15).

Power Up for Connected Learning

Just after the morning bell rings, Avery enters her fifth-grade classroom, greets her tablemates, and begins unloading her backpack. The room buzzes softly with greetings and gentle reminders as students turn in work, organize their materials, do classroom jobs, and shop for books to read in the ample class-room library. Avery snuggles on a couch in the corner of the room with the book she is reading this week. She pauses to send the author a question using the class Twitter account, updates her reading record on Padlet, and jots a few notes for her next blog entry.

Around 9:00 a.m., Katie gathers the students on the carpet for a short read-aloud in which she models strategic reading. Then Avery, Zavier, and Naya read a digital text on the lava flow threatening the village of Pahoa, the current class inquiry, which they have undertaken as a result of their Twitter relationship with a class in Hawaii. Avery and her partners share their thinking as they read, stopping to jot reactions, questions, and observations on a graphic organizer.

Later that morning the class visits its first-grade buddies, who have been reading and responding to the wonder of the day on Wonderopolis. They have captured their thinking with drawings, some students using paper and pencil, others an iPad. The fifth graders are going to teach their buddies how to post these images to their blogs. Avery sits with her buddy, Connor, and coaches him through the process; then she encourages him to write his thinking about the image. (Later Avery and her classmates will comment on these blogs, offering their support and encouragement.)

Back in her classroom, Avery is collaborating on writing a news article tied to the Hawaii inquiry. She works on a Google Doc shared with her writing support circle (Zavier, Naya, and Katie). After listening attentively to the day's focus lesson, she checks her Google Doc for comments and feedback before she begins writing. (At the end of class she will review what her circle mates have done and give them feedback.)

Martina, Naya's first-grade buddy, is back from lunch and getting ready to dig into the day's math work. She is creating a slideshow of her learning from the unit by putting together images she's taken with the classroom digital camera and recording an explanation of what she learned about each activity represented in the image. She ends her short video, edited on a classroom desktop computer, by proudly sharing what she has learned. (Kristin will upload this video to a website where Martina's parents and family members can view her work.)

Students throughout the school move through the day this way, engaged in deep thinking and rich conversation about reading, math, science, social studies, writing, and research. Technology is seamlessly interwoven, and each teacher, regardless of his or her "techpertise," has thought carefully about how and when to use modern technology to enrich, enhance, and amplify students' experiences. Technology is just another tool in students' learning day, one that connects them with their community, supports and furthers their inquiry, and develops the habits and skills of good citizenship through global conversations. Teachers and students see technology as a way to say more, do more, and be more. It's a tool to power up learning!

This chapter suggests some ways you can use technology in the classroom to build reading communities, promote digital discussions, and foster inquiry. The lessons are potential game changers—each not only focuses on amplifying learning with technology but also builds important academic and social skills. Start by building on what you already do to capture student thinking and conversation. Challenge yourself to go beyond just trading a paper-and-pencil option for a technological one. Technology should build on, enhance, and connect learning.

BUILD READING COMMUNITIES

Although we make the case for explicit instruction in reading digitally, our hearts lie in books. The work of Donalyn Miller, Teri Lesesne, Steph Harvey, and Penny Kittle supports our belief that students grow best on a healthy diet of self-selected texts. The sacred moments of our school day are those in which students settle on the classroom couch or stake out a corner of the room and read. We lead by example, sharing ourselves and our reading lives. Our own reading communities and our rich interactions with them have shaped us as readers, and we want to build those same supportive reading communities for our students. We start with the basics ("What are you reading?"), develop their literacy skills (including cultural and technological ones), and ultimately produce a garden of readers, each of whom complements and completes the others.

Photo Book Reviews

What: Capture student thinking about a book he or she is reading with an annotated photo.

Why: Whether shared online or posted in the classroom, these photo book reviews guide readers to books. Students literally see themselves as readers.

How: Using a device's built-in camera and a drawing or annotation tool (like Drawing Pad or Skitch), students annotate a photo of themselves and their favorite book right now. Figure 6.1 shows Jacob with his favorite book, one he authored. It's titled "Ninja vs. Pirate: A Wordless Book." He even awarded himself a Caldecott Medal (yellow circle)! Older students add three words to describe and sell the book to other readers. Photos are shared on a hallway bulletin board or the classroom website.

Wow! When kids reflect on their reading lives and recommend favorite books to other kids, they become a thriving reading community. As part of this process, class members are introduced to a variety of titles and genres. These digital photos can be shared online via a student blog, or classroom Instagram or Twitter account. Using the #readergrams hashtag, students can connect with other kids to share their reading lives.

Figure 6.1 Photo Book Review: Jacob's "Ninja vs. Pirate: A Wordless Book"

Video Book Reviews

What: Students summarize and synthesize their thinking about a book using a combination of text, images, and music.

Why: A video book review is a one-sided conference in which you see and hear kids talk through their thinking about a book. Use them to match books to readers, build book buzz, and share reading lives.

How: Using a device's built-in camera or a more advanced tool like iMovie or WeVideo, students create a video in which they convey details about a book while not giving too much of the story away. Model the process, create a chart identifying important elements to include, and give students plenty of opportunities to practice. Have students share their video book reviews on the classroom website or blog or on Vimeo or YouTube.

Wow! Uploading videos to an online channel ensures that students' work sticks and is accessible beyond the school day and over the course of the year. New audiences can view students' work and appreciate their thinking and learning. When we disseminate video book reviews via a URL, we pair the video clip with a QR code affixed to the cover of the recommended book (see Figure 6.2). As students shop for books in the classroom library, they can scan the QR codes and view book reviews created by kids for kids. Katie's fifth graders sometimes turn their book reviews into book trailers (like movie trailers). They set up a Vimeo channel of their book trailers and book reviews (see Figure 6.3) so that both their classmates and global learning friends can view them.

Twitter and Skype Connections with Authors

What: Students connect with authors of favorite books using tools like Twitter and Skype.

Why: Connecting with authors shows students that writers and illustrators are real people. Their excitement for reading builds, they understand that we are all members of a global learning community, and they see that thinking and learning are fun.

How: There are plenty of authors on both Twitter and Skype, and an Internet search engine will lead you to them. Or check out Kate Messner's list of authors

Figure 6.2 Book Covers with QR Codes

Figure 6.3 Screenshot of Classroom Vimeo Page

who Skype for free (http://bit.ly/1FVx96D) or Joy Kirr's curated list of authors who tweet (http://bit.ly/1Te60Rh). An easy way to get started is by tweeting a question or an appreciation at the end of a read-aloud or during a book club discussion. Setting up a Skype or Google Hangouts meeting introduces students to new options for digital conversation, and many authors are very happy to oblige. Have students prepare questions or comments ahead of time so the session runs smoothly and efficiently.

Wow! These authors can become active members of your learning community. When Katie's students blog about books they're reading, they tweet authors to ask for comments or feedback and provide a link. Tom Angleberger, Rita Williams Garcia, Seymour Simon, and Jenni Holm have all responded. The students see their work as relevant—they have an audience of real readers and their feelings and insights about a book matter. This sense of agency, which Peter Johnston (2004) has written about in depth, inspires students to continue to work, take the next steps in learning, and view the work that they do as significant in and beyond their classroom.

Figure 6.4 Screenshot of a Tweet from Author Matt Holm

Digital Reading "Wall"

What: Replace paper reading logs or "Books I've Read" lists with interactive digital reading walls featuring images, videos, and links.

Why: A digital reading wall is a visual, interactive history of a student's reading over the year. Students build community as they share these walls and their reading lives with classmates and global reading buddies.

How: Using a platform like Padlet, set up a wall on a class account. Model creating a wall and demonstrate how to add a note or a picture. Encourage students to update their digital reading wall whenever they finish a book (establish what students should add, or leave it up to each student).

Wow! Post a photo of each student on a bulletin board with a QR code. Scanning the code will take classmates to a list of books this student has read. Students can also add links to their blog posts, author websites, and other work they've done (book trailers, for example).

Figure 6.5 Each student's photo features a scannable QR code that leads to their personal Padlet of books read for the year. To view an example of a student Padlet, go to: http://padlet.com/302/vivian.

Title Talk for Kids

What: One of the best resources for finding great new titles is the #titletalk Twitter chat monitored by Colby Sharp and Donalyn Miller.

Why: These book chats offer recommendations and suggestions and also teach and support digital discussion skills.

How: Start a #titletalk book chat group in a learning management system like Edmodo. (You can invite students from other classes to join.) Model how to post a comment, and create a list of shared expectations. Make time each week for students to respond or post. You might also have students use the #titletalk hashtag on a classroom Twitter account so that they can interact with teachers and experts.

Wow! Opening your group to students from other schools helps students build global collaboration skills and widen their reading community. It also offers students the opportunity to apply and practice digital communication skills with students outside their classroom community.

ENGAGE IN DIGITAL DISCUSSIONS

When we did our first work with a school in Hawaii, we learned the term *talk story*, which means chatting or shooting the breeze. Friendly exchanges like this, in which we discuss daily happenings and get to know one another, build connections and relationships. Rich, deep, meaningful conversations are also important. Whenever we recommend digital discussions, teachers always want to know:

- How do you keep kids from using text talk?
- How do you make sure they don't say anything inappropriate?
- How do you make sure the quality is rich?

As with everything else we want students to do with independence, we explicitly explain what a digital discussion should look like (see Figure 6.6) and then turn the responsibility and ownership over to our students, teaching and reteaching as we go.

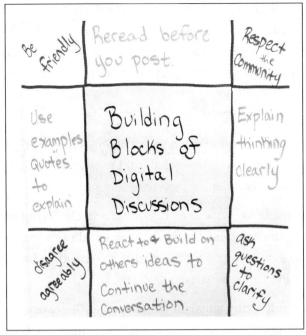

Figure 6.6 Building Blocks of Digital Discussions

Short Text or Image Discussions

What: Students use a digital tool like TodaysMeet, Edmodo, or Padlet to discuss an image or short text.

Why: A digital discussion adds layers to student conversations and interactions. All students can participate, and you and the class can return to and examine the discussion in detail. You can evaluate individual student contributions and the discussion as a whole, and students can reflect on their work. It's a different way for students to share their thinking, the digital version of silent (pen-and-paper) dialogue, and it rounds out our toolbox of instructional techniques.

How: Start with small groups of four, five, or six so student interactions are more manageable. You might have the group members discuss an image, an article, or a picture book. Review your "Guidelines for Digital Discussion" anchor chart, have students introduce themselves, and let them lead the way.

Wow! Wrap up by having students reflect on the discussion face-to-face and perhaps fill out a self-reflection checklist or jot down a quick reflection as an exit ticket. Sometimes we project screenshots of the discussion (see Figure 6.7) and highlight successful strategies or important thinking and then debrief as a class.

Book Club Discussions

What: We aren't suggesting you ditch your students' face-to-face talk in favor of all digital talk, all the time. However, digital exchanges in addition to physical book club meetings add depth.

Why: Students are able to check in as they read, ask clarifying questions, get little details out of the way, and access supplemental texts, images, or videos. These discussions also help you monitor students' reading, interact with them, and share suggestions and resources.

How: If you're already using a learning management network like Edmodo, it's easy to create fluid groups using the small-group function. Otherwise, you can set up a Padlet wall for each group or create rooms on a chat website like TodaysMeet. Schedule time for online posts in class or assign them as homework if all students have access from home. Students should review their digital exchanges and identify key ideas they'd like to discuss in person.

Wow! Students can use these digital discussions in many ways: track their thinking as they read, post photos of the sticky notes they affix to book pages, share favorite lines from the book, or gather ideas to bring to the physical discussion. We sometimes post video clips to pair with the text, author or resource websites to supplement background knowledge, or any current events articles that might relate to the text or topic.

Problem-Solving Discussions

What: Students explore and expand their ability to explain their thinking around math problems in writing through a digital discussion with a small group.

Why: Much of the focus in mathematics these days is on reasoning, proof, and explanation. Digital conversations force students to explain their

Remember we are trying to figure out what is this book really about. What does the character REALLY MEAN when she says that last line?
9:35am, Fri, Jan 9, 2015 by Muhtaris

She means that change can be difficult
9:36am, Fri, Jan 9, 2015 by elijah#Hi

and sometimes its hard to lose things
9:37am, Fri, Jan 9, 2015 by elijah#Hi

I think it's about the time she spent with Matt. And he built it for them.
9:37am, Fri, Jan 9, 2015 by Will

Yeah maybe
9:38am, Fri, Jan 9, 2015 by Vlad

What about the time she spent with him?
9:38am, Fri, Jan 9, 2015 by Muhtaris

Yeah me to I agree with will
9:38am, Fri, Jan 9, 2015 by Nina:)

That's probably why she missed the dugout when they moved
9:39am, Fri, Jan 9, 2015 by Nina:)

I think she means that not everything you do has to be the best and I also think it means that sense they spent a lot of time to built it
9:40am, Fri, Jan 9, 2015 by Leo

ok I think that she is really trying to say that sometimes things don't have to be perfect but it's like your begining is always good
9:40am, Fri, Jan 9, 2015 by Vlad

Yeah it also made a difference that the dugout was made from scratch
9:41am, Fri, Jan 9, 2015 by Nina:)

Agreed
9:41am, Fri, Jan 9, 2015 by Leo

Change ties in with the last line because maybe she wasn't ready for change
9:43am, Fri, Jan 9, 2015 by elijah#Hi

Yeah maybe she got used to having a harder life out in the open
9:44am, Fri, Jan 9, 2015 by Nina:)

Yeah
9:44am, Fri, Jan 9, 2015 by Leooo

That's true. Change can be hard. Don't generalize. What is specific for her about THIS change?
9:44am, Fri, Jan 9, 2015 by Muhtaris

She is not used to it. Maybe she likes the dugout better now that she thinks about it
9:46am, Fri, Jan 9, 2015 by Nina:)

Maybe she dose not feel like her new house is like home. After she has lived in the dugout so long that's what she thinks as home
9:48am, Fri, Jan 9, 2015 by Nina:)

i think maybe the change was a little hard since they lived there for so long and now they have to leave so that is why she was all like tha
9:48am, Fri, Jan 9, 2015 by Vlad

"built a clapboard house with windows like suns, floors I slipped on, and the empty sound of too many rooms."
9:49am, Fri, Jan 9, 2015 by Muhtaris

I also realize matts cave which was the cave in the earth so I thought maybe Matt always wanted.....
9:49am, Fri, Jan 9, 2015 by Suiyee

To live there
9:49am, Fri, Jan 9, 2015 by Suiyee

Yeah
9:49am, Fri, Jan 9, 2015 by $Vlad$

She dose not like her new house ? Muhtaris
9:49am, Fri, Jan 9, 2015 by Nina:)

I think having happy memories and being with people you care about makes a house a home
9:50am, Fri, Jan 9, 2015 by Ella

I agree Ella
9:50am, Fri, Jan 9, 2015 by Suiyee

Figure 6.7 Excerpt of a Student Discussion on TodaysMeet

thinking clearly and also help them see when words just won't do and a model is necessary to tell the story.

How: Form small groups of three or four students. Post a problem for students to discuss using the process described in Figure 6.8 (the goal is explanations, not just answers). Everyone in the group must agree on the final answer and understand how it was obtained. Provide a chart of helpful problem-solving language and sentence stems for students to refer to. Model the process by having students observe a live discussion.

Wow! When students are sitting close together, they can move spontaneously between digital and face-to-face interaction. Play with groupings, formats, and types of problems. Encourage students to post pictures or drawings of their work and share screencasts with one another.

* Talk through the problem with the other members of your group; determine what you are supposed to find out.
* Share steps you think you should take to solve the problem.
* Solve the problem together, reading and replying to other group members' comments.
* If you agree, say or show why.
* If you disagree, explain why politely.
* Agree on the answer as a group.

Figure 6.8 How to Talk About Problems in a Digital Discussion

Conversation in the Comments

What: One of our students once described the comments section of a blog as a place to leave a digital sticky note for the writer (Harvey et al. 2013). We love that analogy and encourage kids to comment on articles and classmates' blog posts.

Why: Spontaneous digital discussion in a comments section is both authentic and validating. It's also valuable practice for using digital media in the real world.

How: Begin by teaching students how to leave thoughtful comments connected to what they are reading, give supportive and constructive feedback, and ask questions that spur discussion and dialogue. Then teach them how to respond to comments left on their work and jump into discussions by responding to comments left on other blogs. Model, guide, and support.

Wow! Commenting skills go a long way in building community and producing digital citizens who value respectful and sometimes spirited conversation. Once students are well practiced, have them explore blogs in addition to those of their classmates, as well as the comments sections of websites like Wonderopolis and *TweenTribune*.

Cross-Classroom Discussions

What: Create an opportunity for global collaboration by hosting a digital discussion that involves students from other classrooms, schools, or countries.

Why: Although there are many diverse viewpoints in your classroom, having digital conversations with students in other classrooms introduces varied opinions and fresh perspectives. Global classroom discussions connect kids to a wider audience for their ideas and build connections among classrooms, communities, and countries.

How: Start small by collaborating with the teacher of a classroom down the hall. As you become more comfortable, expand to classrooms in other schools, states, and countries. Find a collaborative tool that works well for both classrooms—Edmodo, a Twitter hashtag, a blog, or some other interactive Web-based tool. Set shared expectations. Then dig in. Responding to a shared read-aloud is a good place to start: both teachers read the same book aloud and students respond. You can also join established communities like Mystery Skype (@MysterySkype, http://bit.ly/1iVmaOQ) or Global Read Aloud (http://bit.ly/1e62Dfm).

Wow! Once students begin building relationships with one another, consider more in-depth coordination: cross-classroom book clubs and problem solving or acquainting one another with their respective communities and cultures. Older students can engage in activism around shared topics and issues of interest. The possibilities are endless.

FOSTER INQUIRY ACROSS THE CURRICULUM

Student inquiry is an essential part of our day. "What do you wonder? Where can we go to find more information? Why does this matter?" It's also a huge topic beyond the scope of this book. Check out *Comprehension and Collaboration* (Harvey and Daniels 2009) or *Learning for Real* (Mills 2014) to learn the details of an inquiry approach to learning. The lessons here are small steps to get you started.

Provide a Space for Wonder

What: Create physical and digital spaces to hold student questions so that you can revisit and research them during the year.

Why: Stephanie Harvey says that passion, wonder, and curiosity are the cornerstone of the elementary curriculum. Every student can wonder. Young children don't need much inspiration to wonder about the world; it's older students who often lose the art of curiosity in the classroom. We need to encourage children's natural curiosity as it develops a passion for learning, provides a real-world context for the skills we teach, and nurtures children's desire to understand the world around them.

Figure 6.9 A Pre-K Student Shares Her Wonder About the iPad

How: Text, images, videos, ephemera, maps, brochures, infographics—almost anything can be a starting point for wonder. Provide a space to hold wonderings (either a real or a digital bulletin board works nicely; see Figures 6.9 and 6.10). Although we want kids to wonder all day, every day, we often have to carve out a starting place. We love using the website Wonderopolis to ignite curiosity. In the beginning, designate a special time; we have Wonder Wednesdays and use the hashtag #wonderwednesday to tweet our wonders and our work related to them. Model your own wonderings and then invite students to join you.

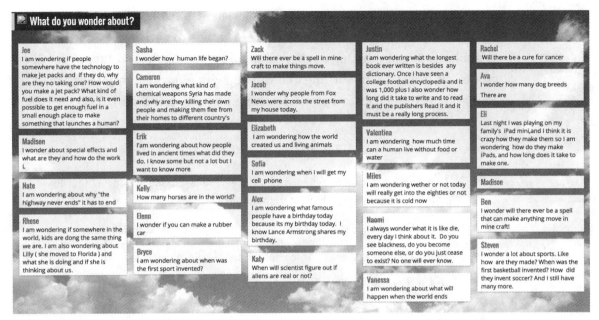

What do you wonder about?

Joe
I am wondering if people somewhere have the technology to make jet packs and if they do, why are they no taking one? How would you make a jet pack? What kind of fuel does it need and also, is it even possible to get enough fuel in a small enough place to make something that launches a human?

Madison
I wonder about special effects and what are they and how do the work
L

Nate
I am wondering about why "the highway never ends" it has to end

Rhese
I am wondering if somewhere in the world, kids are dong the same thing we are. I am also wondering about Lilly (she moved to Florida) and what she is doing and if she is thinking about us.

Sasha
I wonder how human life began?

Cameron
I am wondering what kind of chemical weapons Syria has made and why are they killing their own people and making them flee from their homes to different country's

Erik
I'am wondering about how people lived in ancient times what did they do. I know some but not a lot but I want to know more

Kelly
How many horses are in the world?

Elenn
I wonder if you can make a rubber car

Bryce
I am wondering about when was the first sport invented?

Zack
Will there ever be a spell in mine-craft to make things move.

Jacob
I wonder why people from Fox News were across the street from my house today.

Elizabeth
I am wondering how the world created us and living animals

Sofia
I am wondering when I will get my cell phone

Alex
I am wondering what famous people have a birthday today because its my birthday today. I know Lance Armstrong shares my birthday.

Katy
When will scientist figure out if aliens are real or not?

Justin
I am wondering what the longest book ever written is besides any dictionary. Once I have seen a college football encyclopedia and it was 1,000 plus I also wonder how long did it take to write and to read it and the publishers Read it and it must be a really long process.

Valentina
I am wondering how much time can a human live without food or water

Miles
I am wondering wether or not today will really get into the eighties or not because it is cold now

Naomi
I always wonder what it is like die, every day I think about it. Do you see blackness, do you become someone else, or do you just cease to exist? No one will ever know.

Vanessa
I am wondering about what will happen when the world ends

Rachel
Will there be a cure for cancer

Ava
I wonder how many dog breeds
There are

Eli
Last night I was playing on my family's iPad mini,and I think it is crazy how they make them so I am wondering how do they make iPads, and how long does it take to make one.

Madison

Ben
I wonder will there ever be a spell that can make anything move in mine craft!

Steven
I wonder a lot about sports. Like how are they made? When was the first basketball invented? How did they invent soccer? And I still have many more.

Figure 6.10 A Digital Wonder Wall

Wow! Student wonderings shouldn't live only in notebooks, on bulletin boards, or in tweets. They need to be given life through follow-up—asking, reading, researching, sharing. They are starting points for authentic reading, interviewing, writing, and investigating. Students embrace the cycle of wonderment: ask questions, find answers, ask even more questions. To power up the experience, connect with classrooms around the globe: wonder and research together, collaborate on a piece of writing, and make friends in the process.

Inspire Wonder Through Images or Artifacts

What: Use images and artifacts as a catalyst for inspiring student questions and thinking.

Why: Images are powerful sources of wonder, whether for primary students fascinated by the pictures of animals on a calendar or older students examining political cartoons. An image—or any object students manipulate, explore, and play with, question what it is and what it might be used for, and want to find out more about—is the perfect starting point for wonder. Every student can access the learning.

How: First, model how to view an image or an artifact. Look at both the big picture and the little details. Use a chart of things to notice (see Figure 6.11) to guide students' thinking as they respond by talking face-to-face in small groups or as a class, by turning and talking with a partner, by jotting notes on a graphic organizer, or by collaborating digitally (see Figure 6.12).

* Notice the big picture. When and where is this taking place? What do you see? What do you think is happening?

* Look at the small details; zoom in on little parts of the image.

* Notice colors, placement, or composition of the elements in the picture.

* Look for text or writing in the image.

Figure 6.11 Things to Notice

* Show an image or artifact and model some noticing strategies. Have students turn and talk about what they notice.

* Show an image or artifact and have students jot their thinking in a notebook or on a clipboard, occasionally turning and talking with a partner and sharing as a group.

* Have students view images taped to chart paper and respond in writing on the chart, chatting as they do.

* Have students examine artifacts at learning stations, capturing their thoughts on sticky notes or scanning a QR code that opens a Padlet wall where they can post their thoughts.

* Have students view images on a classroom computer or tablet and respond on a graphic organizer.

* Have students view images posted to a blog or classroom social media site and respond in the comments section.

Figure 6.12 Structures for Analyzing Images and Artifacts

Wow! Power up this experience by working with local museums. Many museums provide boxes of artifacts that can be checked out, and most have special guided tours for students. Katie's students spent a morning examining ancient Greek artifacts at the National Hellenic Museum after examining images of artifacts in class. These experiences helped them develop shared language, refined their observational skills, and enriched their informational writing.

Inspire Wonder Through Video Clips

What: Inspire kids by using short video clips to introduce, reinforce, or expand on a topic of thinking.

Why: As we reimagine what it means to read, we need to explicitly teach our students to evaluate, comprehend, critique, and question print and nonprint sources. Bringing infographics, music, still images, and video into our classrooms enhances text, inspires curiosity, and differentiates instruction for multimodal learners.

How: View short video clips that inspire wonder and curiosity. Sites such as The Kid Should See This (http://bit.ly/1q3jhNJ) contain many student-friendly, seriously interesting media clips. Watch them several times. First, watch the entire clip. During repeated viewings, closely read the videos and pause to wonder and jot down questions. Model inferring from and asking questions about media. Provide opportunities for students to determine important information and synthesize it. Video clips bring the world into your classroom and provide opportunities for students to wonder about places, phenomena, and situations they may not encounter in their daily life. Explicitly teach students how to view them with a wide-awake mind, annotate them, and share their thinking with a peer.

Wow! The third graders that Kristin works with produce a monthly podcast that features a segment on wonder. Using iMovie, students create their own wonder videos modeled after The Kid Should See This. After the podcast is released, the other classrooms in the school research the wonder and continue the discussion on social media for the next few weeks. Viewing to wonder becomes a thread that connects the school community.

Collaborate Digitally to Gather, Organize, and Share Questions for Inquiry

What: When we begin a unit of study, we often have students, in small teams, brainstorm questions to guide their learning.

Why: A digital format makes these sessions easy to organize and archive and offers better access to all learners.

How: Use a digital collaboration tool such as Google Docs, Padlet, or Todays-Meet to set up a place for students to share questions and wonderings. (Todays-Meet is a great way for students to share their questions publicly; Google Docs provides more freedom in categorizing, editing, and updating questions over the course of the unit.) Use a projector to share the document with the class as students work (or after the fact if you are having students brainstorm in small groups). Use this as a jumping-off point for your inquiry, tying classroom experiences to student questions and wonderings.

Wow! Once you've established this strategy, students can apply it in their small-group inquiries. Have students collaborate digitally on all aspects of their work—division of labor, list of resources used, work plans and calendars, supply lists . . . whatever needs doing. Work done digitally is easy to share with teachers, support personnel, and parents. Katie puts students in inquiry groups based on interest. Then she creates a chart on Google Docs on which students compile a list of subtopics and questions to guide their research (see Figure 6.13). Student groups collaborate face-to-face and digitally to brainstorm, organize, and finalize their questions. Figure 6.14 shows the questions one group generated.

Create Inquiry Trailers

What: Students create multimedia presentations to archive and reflect on the inquiry process from brainstorming questions to going public.

Why: When students become immersed in a longer inquiry, especially one tied to a unit of study, the focus often shifts to creating the product instead of honoring the process of asking, learning, and asking again. Inquiry trailers encourage students to curate the process of learning bit by bit, day by day.

Guiding Question	Follow-Up Questions
What was daily life like for Ancient Greeks?	**Examples** ❑ What kinds of clothes did people wear? Where did the material come from? Did everyone get the same kind of clothes? ❑ How was your day to day impacted by your job or social status? <Your team will fill in the rest.>
What was it like to be an Ancient Greek warrior?	❑ What types of uniforms were there? What weapons did they use? ❑ What was life like for Spartan warriors? <Your team will fill in the rest.>
What happened in the city of Pompeii?	❑ Why is the city of Pompeii important to us today? <Your team will fill in the rest.>
What would it have been like to be a gladiator?	❑ Who were the gladiators? ❑ What kinds of battles did they have? <Your team will fill in the rest.>
What was the Roman army like?	❑ What types of uniforms were there? What weapons did they use? ❑ Who did they conquer? <Your team will fill in the rest.>

Figure 6.13 Class Inquiry Question Chart

What was daily life like in Ancient Rome?	**Examples** ❑ What kinds of clothes did people wear? Where did the material come from? Did everyone get the same kind of clothes? ❑ How was your day to day impacted by your job or social status? ❑ Clothing and accessories ❑ What type of clothing did they wear? ❑ How did they wear their hair? ❑ What type of jewelry did they have and makeup? ❑ Was the clothing in Rome close to Greece? **Food** ❑ When and where did they eat their meals? ❑ What did they eat for breakfast, lunch, and dinner? ❑ What types of drinks did they have besides wine? ❑ What did women bake? ❑ How often did they have feasts or festivals?	**Houses** ❑ Who had what type of house? ❑ Were all houses temples? ❑ What were their house decorations? **Miscellaneous** ❑ How old do you have to be to get married? ❑ How often did they go to the beach? ❑ Who built the Coliseum? ❑ What kind of sports did they play? ❑ What were the laws? ❑ Where were the toilets located? ❑ What types of pets did they have? ❑ What was their way of transportation? ❑ How many people can go in a bath at a time? ❑ What is the rich/poor schedule? ❑ What types of war did they have? **School** ❑ Did they write letters? ❑ What were their schools like? ❑ Who went to school?

Figure 6.14 Group Inquiry Question Chart for Daily Life in Ancient Rome

How: At the beginning of an inquiry cycle or unit, ask students to video record a small moment each day as a reminder of the important work they are doing. These should be tied to what we value in the inquiry process: questions the group asked, books and resources they used, things they learned, successes and challenges, images of works in progress, snapshots of group members working. At the end of the cycle students can quickly combine these images using a movie app and set it to music. They finish up by adding a few slides listing major takeaways and lingering questions.

Wow! These inquiry stories are a window into your students' process. They can be short (e.g., "Show the six most important moments in your process.") or take on longer lives of their own. When students go public with their learning, they can share their inquiry movie as part of the final product, demonstrating that the process was just as important as the final product.

A FEW WORDS IN CONCLUSION

A journey begins with just one step.
         —Buddha

We build our teaching lives brick-by-brick, step-by-step. Choose one thing, just one, and start there. It doesn't matter where you are on the continuum of learning as long as you're willing to learn. Commit to discovering one new thing each quarter. Chances are you'll learn more than one new thing in those ten weeks, and by the end of the school year you'll have a variety of new tools and practices that you'll be using with students. Take that step. Lay the first brick. Before you know it, you'll have a foundation to build on and a structure for thinking and learning digitally.

 Scan this QR code or visit http://hein.pub/amplify to see videos of teachers and students in action and access up-to-date resources for this book (use keycode AMPLIFY15).

Works Cited

Boston Children's Museum. n.d. "The Power of Play." Boston Children's Museum. Accessed January 3, 2015, at www.bostonchildrensmuseum.org/power-of-play.

Calkins, Lucy and colleagues. 2010. *Units of Study for Teaching Reading, Grades 3–5: A Curriculum for the Reading Workshop.* Portsmouth, NH: Heinemann.

Carroll, Kevin. 2013. "Play Is . . . ." Lecture presented at TEDxRVA, Richmond, VA, June 20.

Coiro, Julie. 2011. "Predicting Reading Comprehension on the Internet: Contributions of Offline Reading Skills, Online Reading Skills, and Prior Knowledge." *Journal of Literacy Research* 43 (4): 352–92.

Devany, Laura. 2014. "Screen Time Debate Broadens with Research." *eSchool News*, October 27. Accessed December 4, 2014, at www.eschoolnews.com/2014/10/27/screen -time-research-039.

Fondas, Nanette. 2014. "Study: You Really Can 'Work Smarter, Not Harder.'" *The Atlantic* online, May 15. Accessed January 22, 2015, at www.theatlantic.com/education/archive /2014/05/study-you-really-can-work-smarter-not-harder/370819/.

Fountas, Irene, and Gay Su Pinnell. 2000. *Guiding Readers and Writers.* Portsmouth, NH: Heinemann.

Goble, Don. 2014. "Defining What Broadcast Means for Scholastic Journalism." JEA Digital Media, December 4. Accessed January 2, 2015, at www.jeadigitalmedia.org/2014 /12/04/defining-what-broadcast-means-for-scholastic-journalism.

Golinkoff, Roberta, and Kathy Hirsch-Pasek. 2014. "Active, Engaged, Meaningful and Interactive: Putting the 'Education' Back in Educational Apps." *The Huffington Post* online, January 10. Accessed December 22, 2014, at www.huffingtonpost.com/roberta-michnick -golinkoff/putting-the-education-back-in-educational-apps_b_4571859.html.

Harvey, Stephanie, and Harvey Daniels. 2009. *Comprehension and Collaboration: Inquiry Circles in Action.* Portsmouth, NH: Heinemann.

Harvey, Stephanie, and Anne Goudvis. 2005. *The Comprehension Toolkit: Language and Lessons for Active Literacy.* Portsmouth, NH: Heinemann.

———. 2007. *Strategies That Work.* 2nd ed. Portland, ME: Stenhouse.

———. 2013. "Comprehension at the Core." *Reading Teacher* 66 (6): 432–39.

Harvey, Stephanie, Anne Goudvis, Katie Muhtaris, and Kristin Ziemke. 2013. *Connecting Comprehension and Technology: Adapt and Extend Toolkit Practices*. Portsmouth, NH: Heinemann.

Johnston, Peter H. 2004. *Choice Words: How Our Language Affects Children's Learning*. Portland, ME: Stenhouse.

Kanani, Rahim. 2014. "The Transformative Power of Play and Its Link to Creativity." *Forbes online*, January 25. Accessed May 13, 2015, at www.forbes.com/sites /rahimkanani/2014/01/25/the-transformative-power-of-play-and-its-link-to -creativity/.

Konnikova, Maria. 2014. "Being a Better Online Reader." *The New Yorker* online, July 16. Accessed December 3, 2014, at www.newyorker.com/science/maria-konnikova/being -a-better-online-reader.

Lehman, Christopher, and Kate Roberts. 2014. *Falling in Love with Close Reading*. Portsmouth, NH: Heinemann.

Lesesne, Teri S. 2010. *Reading Ladders: Leading Students from Where They Are to Where We'd Like Them to Be*. Portsmouth, NH: Heinemann.

Light, Daniel, and Deborah Keisch Polin. 2010. *Integrating Web 2.0 Tools into the Classroom: Changing the Culture of Learning*. New York: EDC Center for Children and Technology. Accessed March 2, 2015, at http://cct.edc.org/sites/cct.edc.org/files /publications/Integrating Web2.0.PDF.

Marano, Hara Estroff. 1999. "The Power of Play." *Psychology Today* online, July 1. Accessed November 2, 2014, at www.psychologytoday.com/articles/199907/the-power -play.

Martinelli, Marjorie, and Kristine Mraz. 2012. *Smarter Charts, K–2: Optimizing an Instructional Staple to Create Independent Readers and Writers*. Portsmouth, NH: Heinemann.

Martinez, Sylvia Libow, and Gary Stager. *Invent to Learn: Making, Tinkering, and Engineering in the Classroom*. Torrance, CA: Constructing Modern Knowledge.

Mathers, Brandi Gribble, and Amanda J. Stern. 2012. "Café Culture: Promoting Empowerment and Pleasure in Adolescent Literacy Learning." *Reading Horizons* 51 (4): 259–78.

Miller, Debbie. 2013. *Reading with Meaning: Teaching Comprehension in the Primary Grades*. 2d ed. Portland, ME: Stenhouse.

Miller, Donalyn. 2009. *The Book Whisperer: Awakening the Inner Reader in Every Child*. San Francisco: Jossey-Bass.

Miller, Donalyn, and Susan Kelley. 2013. *Reading in the Wild: The Book Whisperer's Keys to Cultivating Lifelong Reading Habits*. San Francisco: Jossey-Bass.

Mills, Heidi. 2014. *Learning for Real: Teaching Content and Literacy Across the Curriculum*. Portsmouth, NH: Heinemann.

Moeller, Babette, and Tim Reitzes. 2011. *Integrating Technology with Student-Centered Learning.* Quincy, MA: Nellie Mae Education Foundation. Accessed March 31, 2015, at www.nmefoundation.org/research/personalization/integrating-technology-with-student-centered-learn.

Nagy, William, Patricia Herman, and Richard Anderson. 1985. "Learning Words from Context." *Reading Research Quarterly* 20 (2): 233–53.

National Institute for Play website. Carmel Valley, CA: National Institute for Play. Accessed January 22, 2015, at www.nifplay.org.

Newman, Bobbi. 2010. "What Is Transliteracy?" *Libraries and Transliteracy* (blog), February 16. Accessed February 3, 2015, at https://librariesandtransliteracy.wordpress.com/what-is-transliteracy.

Nichols, Maria. 2006. *Comprehension Through Conversation: The Power of Purposeful Talk in the Reading Workshop.* Portsmouth, NH: Heinemann.

Nielson, Jakob. 2006. "F-Shaped Pattern for Reading Web Content." Nielsen Norman Group, April 17. Accessed July 22, 2014, at www.nngroup.com/articles/f-shaped-pattern-reading-web-content.

November, Alan C. 2012. *Who Owns the Learning? Preparing Students for Success in the Digital Age.* Bloomington, IN: Solution Tree.

Pahamov, Larissa. 2014. "Making Reflection Relevant." In *Authentic Learning in the Digital Age: Engaging Students Through Inquiry.* Alexandria, VA: ASCD.

Pearson, P. David, and Janice A. Dole. 1987. "Explicit Comprehension Instruction: A Review of Research and a New Conceptualization of Instruction." *Elementary School Journal* 88: 151–65.

Puentedura, Ruben R. n.d. *Ruben R. Puentedura's Weblog.* Accessed March 30, 2015, at www.hippasus.com/rrpweblog.

Rami, Meenoo. 2014. *Thrive: 5 Ways to (Re)invigorate Your Teaching.* Portsmouth, NH: Heinemann.

Schugar, Heather Ruetschlin, Carol A. Smith, and Jordan T. Schugar. 2013. "Teaching with Interactive Picture E-books in Grades K–6." *The Reading Teacher* 66 (8): 615–24.

Serravallo, Jennifer, and Gravity Goldberg. 2007. *Conferring with Readers: Supporting Each Student's Growth and Independence.* Portsmouth, NH: Heinemann.

Shear, Linda, Larry Gallagher, and Deepa Patel. 2011. "Innovative Teaching and Learning Research: 2011 Findings and Implications." Accessed June 3, 2015, at www.sri.com/work/publications/innovative-teaching-and-learning-research-2011-findings-and-implications.

Shellenbarger, Sue. 2014. "The Power of the Doodle: Improve Your Focus and Memory." *Wall Street Journal* online, July 29. Accessed February 14, 2015, at www.wsj.com/articles/the-power-of-the-doodle-improve-your-focus-and-memory-1406675744.

Tabor, Sharon W., and Robert Minch. 2013. "Student Adoption and Development of Digital Learning Media: Action Research and Recommended Practices." *Journal of Information Technology Education* 12: 203–23.

Toyama, Kentaro. 2015. "Technology Won't Fix America's Neediest Schools. It Makes Bad Education Worse." *The Washington Post* online, June 4. Accessed June 8, 2015, at http://www.washingtonpost.com/posteverything/wp/2015/06/04/technology-wont -fix-americas-neediest-schools-it-makes-bad-education-worse/.

Vega, Vanessa. 2013. "Technology Integration Research Review." Edutopia, February 5. Accessed March 31, 2015, at www.edutopia.org/technology-integration-research -learning-outcomes#outcomes.

Zemelman, Steven, Harvey Daniels, and Arthur Hyde. 2012. *Best Practice: Bringing Standards to Life in America's Classrooms*. 4th ed. Portsmouth, NH: Heinemann.

KATIE MUHTARIS • KRISTIN ZIEMKE

AMPLIFY

Digital Teaching and Learning in the K–6 Classroom

Foreword by STEPHANIE HARVEY

HEINEMANN
Portsmouth, NH

Heinemann
361 Hanover Street
Portsmouth, NH 03801–3912
www.heinemann.com

Offices and agents throughout the world

The authors and publisher wish to thank those who have generously given permission to reprint borrowed material:

Page 3: Photograph © Kelly van Dellen/Shutterstock

Figure 1.6 (*clockwise*): © Hung Chung Chih/Shutterstock/HIP; © QiangBa DanZhen/Fotolia/ HIP; © Photodisc/Getty Images/HIP; © Tan Kian Khoon/Shutterstock

Figure 2.1: WordPress screenshot created by Katie Muhtaris, www.wordpress.com. Used in accordance with the Creative Commons Attribution-ShareAlike License 4.0, http:// creativecommons.org/licenses/by-sa/4.0/.

Cover and interior pages from *Bones* by Steve Jenkins. Text and art copyright © 2010 by Steve Jenkins. Reprinted by permission of Scholastic Inc.

Cataloging-in-Publication Data is on file at the Library of Congress.
ISBN: 978-0-325-07473-3

Editor: Holly Kim Price
Developmental editor: Alan Huisman
Production: Victoria Merecki
Typesetter: Kim Arney
Cover and interior designs: Suzanne Heiser
Video production: Sherry Day and Michael Grover
Manufacturing: Steve Bernier

Printed in the United States of America on acid-free paper

19   18   17   16   VP   3   4   5